iPhone™ 3G
Made Simple

Includes New 3.0 Software
Upgrade Process and Features

Another in the
***Made Simple*™**
Guide Book Series

By
Martin Trautschold
Gary Mazo

iPhone® 3G
Made Simple

This book is intended to help owners of the iPhone 3G 8GB and 16GB with version 2.2 and 3.0 software.

Please check out our electronic versions at
www.MadeSimpleLearning.com

Published by
CMT Publications, Inc.
25 Forest View Way
Ormond Beach, FL 32174

ISBN-10: 1-4392-4638-6
ISBN-13: 978-1-4392-4638-2
Published Date: July 25, 2009

Published in the United States of America

10 9 8 7 6 5 4 3 2 1

Trademark Acknowledgements

Images
iPhone images courtesy of Apple, inc. (www.apple.com)

Contact Us
Contact the authors at info@MadeSimpleLearning.com For Free Email Tips, and the Electronic Version ("E-book") in Adobe PDF format, please visit
www.MadeSimpleLearning.com

Contents at a Glance

Table of Contents

Check out our web site at www.MadeSimpleLearning.com

Authors & Acknowledgements

 **Martin Trautschold** is the Founder and CEO of Made Simple Learning, a leading provider of Smartphone Training Videos and Books, primarily for RIM BlackBerry Smartphones. We are now using our proven training techniques for the iPhone, iPod Touch and Palm Pre devices. He has been a successful entrepreneur in the smartphone training and software business for the past nine years. With Made Simple Learning, he has been helping to train thousands of BlackBerry users with short, to-the-point video tutorials. He has also co-authored nine BlackBerry-related "Made Simple" guide books. Gary Mazo has been Martin's co-author on all the most recent books. Martin and Gary teamed up with Kevin Michaluk, founder of CrackBerry.com to write a part-serious, part-funny, but wholly entertaining guide to BlackBerry addiction called: "CrackBerry: True Tales of BlackBerry Use and Abuse."

Martin began his entrepreneurial life with a wireless software company which he co-founded with his brother-in-law, Ned Johnson. Together, they spent 3 years growing it and then sold it, the company's flagship product "Handheld Contact" is still being developed, marketed and sold by the new owners. Martin also has 15 years experience managing complex technology and business projects for consulting, technology and energy firms in the US and Japan. He holds a Bachelor of Science in Engineering Degree from Princeton University and an MBA from the Kellogg School at Northwestern University. In his "free time" he enjoys spending time with his wife, Julie, and three children. Occasionally, he tries to sneak a few hours to row on the Halifax River with his daughter or ride his bicycle with friends in Ormond Beach, Florida. Martin can be reached at martin@madesimplelearning.com.

> I would like to thank my co-author Gary Mazo for his tireless effort in helping to make this book a success. This book is much more comprehensive due to his efforts. Special thanks goes out to all the Made Simple Learning customers who have asked great questions and shared their tips, many of which are in this book! I would also like to thank my wife, Julie and my daughters for their support over the many months of writing, re-writing and editing.
>
>   -- Martin Trautschold

 **Gary Mazo** is a writer, a College Professor, a gadget nut and an ordained rabbi. Gary joined Made Simple Learning in 2007 and has co - authored the last seven books in the Made Simple Learning Series. He serves as VP of the company as well. Along with Martin and Kevin Michaluk from CrackBerry.com, Gary co-wrote "CrackBerry: True Tales of BlackBerry Use and Abuse" - a book about BlackBerry addiction and how to get a grip on one's BlackBerry use.

Gary also teaches at the University of Phoenix – teaching Writing, Philosophy, Technical Writing and more. Gary is a regular contributor to CrackBerry.com – writing product reviews and adding editorial content. Gary is also the Director of Kollel of Cape Cod – a cutting edge Jewish Educational institution/Congregation in Marstons Mills, Massachusetts. He holds a BA in Anthropology from Brandeis University. Gary earned his M.A.H.L (Masters in Hebrew Letters) as well as ordination as Rabbi from the Hebrew Union College-Jewish Institute of Religion in Cincinnati, Ohio. He has served congregations in Dayton, Ohio; Cherry Hill, New Jersey; and Hyannis, Massachusetts.

His first book, entitled "And the Flames Did Not Consume Us" achieved critical acclaim and was published by Rising Star Press in 2000.

Gary is married to Gloria Schwartz Mazo and between them, they have six children. Gary can be reached at: gary@madesimplelearning.com.

> This book is only possible due to the support of several individuals in my life. First, I would like to thank Martin Trautschold for giving me the opportunity to join him in this project. Next, I want to thank my wife, Gloria and our kids; Ari, Dan, Sara, Bill, Elise and Jonah – without whom I would not have the support to pursue projects like this one.

> -- Gary Mazo

Other Made Simple Learning Products

Formerly BlackBerry Made Simple

Books:
CrackBerry: True Tales of BlackBerry® Use and Abuse
BlackBerry Curve™ 8350i *Made Simple*
BlackBerry Pearl™ 'Flip' 8200 *Made Simple*
BlackBerry Bold™ 9000 *Made Simple (coming soon)*
BlackBerry Curve™ 8900*Made Simple (coming soon)*
BlackBerry Pearl *Made Simple* for 8100 Series
  BlackBerry smartphones
BlackBerry 8300/8800 Series *Made Simple*
BlackBerry *Made Simple*™ for Full Keyboard BlackBerry
  smartphones (87xx, 77xx, 75xx, 72xx, 6xxx Series)
BlackBerry *Made Simple*™ for 7100 Series BlackBerry
  smartphones (7100, 7130, 71xx Series)

Videos Now™
(Viewed On Your Computer)
We offer a full library of over 350 3-minute video
training clips for all popular BlackBerry models. As of
publishing time, we are exploring the possibility of
creating similar videos for the iPhone and iPod Touch.

Videos To Go™
Video Training You Watch on your Smartphone
Video training you download watch right on your
Smartphone. As of publishing time, we are exploring
the possibility of creating similar videos for the
iPhone and iPod Touch.

VideosToGo™
Mobile Video Training
About Your BlackBerry
On Your BlackBerry

Quick Reference Guide

Getting Started

The items below will help you get up and running with your iPhone.

To Do This...	Use This...	Where to Learn More
Turn on or off the iPhone	Power / Sleep Key	Press and hold this key on the top. Page 36
Start the Phone, Place a Call	Phone Icon	Page 102
Turn off the Ringer	Ringer / Mute Switch	Slide this key to Mute / Un-Mute. Page 32
Check Voicemail	Voicemail Icon	Page 111
Use the Camera	Camera Icon	Page 131
Send a Text Message	SMS icon	Page 146
Buy Music	iTunes Icon	Page 320

To Do This...	Use This...		Where to Learn More
Return to Home Screen		**Home Button**	Page 36
Unlock Your iPhone	**Slide to Unlock**		Page 41
Completely Power Down Your iPhone	**Press & Hold Power Key**	**Then slide...**	Page 36
Start Listening to Music		**iPod icon**	Page 169
Sync Music, Videos, Pictures, Addresses, Calendar, Email and Notes with your Computer	**iTunes (for Windows™) and Apple™ Mac™)**		Page 62
Start Watching Videos		**Videos**	Page 188
Surf the Web		**Safari**	Page 201

Stay Organized

Use these things to stay in organized with your iPhone.

To Do This...	Use This...		Where to Learn More
Manage Your Contact Names & Numbers		Contacts	Basics – Page 246
Manage your Calendar		Calendar	Basics - Page 255 Sync to PC or Mac - Page 92
Take notes, store your grocery list and more!		Notes	Basics - Page 296 Sync to PC or Mac - Page 95
Look at, Manage, Organize your Pictures		Photos	Page 270
View & Send Email		Mail	Page 228
Calculate your MPG, a meal tip, and more!		Calculator	Other Applications Page 314
Set a wakeup alarm, use a countdown timer or stopwatch		Clock	Page 306
Adjust all Important Settings for the Device		Settings	Page 165
Find just about Anything, get Directions		Maps	Page 282

Be Entertained

Use these things to have fun with your iPhone!

To Do This...	Use This...	Where to Learn More
Quickly get to all your Music!	**Music**	Page 176
See Playlists,Artists,Songs, Albums, Audiobooks and more..	**Music**	Playlists – Page 171 Artists – Page 173 Songs – Page 174 Albums– Page 174
Look at, Zoom in and Organize your Pictures	**Photos**	Page 269
Watch Movies and Music Videos	**Videos**	Page 188
Take a Break and Play a Game	**Games Icons**	Page 339
Browse and Download Apps right to your iPhone	**App Store**	Page 338

Learning Your iPhone:
The Screen, Buttons, Switches and Ports

Signal Strength Indicator
Number of Bars (strength)
And Data Connection
Indicator.
Shows Signal Strength and
connection status: 3G (high
speed), E (lower speed) and
Wi-Fi (high speed) Status

Headphone
Jack

Wake/Sleep – On/Off Button
Tap to go to sleep or wake up,
press & hold to power on or off.

Bluetooth Indicator
Shows Bluetooth
is enabled.

Ringer On/Off
"Mute" Switch

Volume Up &
Down Keys

Battery Strength
TIP: Charge every
night, especially if
you are on the
phone, browse the
web or use 3G a lot.

Bottom Dock
These icons are always visible.
Press and hold an icon to
move it down to this dock.

Search & Dots
In 3.0 software, you will
see a magnifying glass to
the left of the 'dots' – your
"SEARCH" screen. Each
dot represents a screen of
icons. Swipe left/right.

"Home" Button
Press from any
Application to return to
the Home Screen

Charging/Sync Port
Connect to PC or MAC
To Sync Music, Contacts
and more with iTunes

Knowing When You are Connected

There are some letters and symbols in the upper left corner of your iPhone that tell you whether you are connected for data (e.g. email, web browsing and downloading apps) or just your phone and SMS text messaging.

TIP: If your data connectivity is not working well, then try turning Airplane Mode on and off (See next page.) If that does not help, then try turning your iPhone off then on. Finally, if you need more help then try some of the troubleshooting tips found in our "Fixing Problems" chapter on page 355.

Signal Strength & Data Connectivity Letters

AT&T Network (USA)

...ıll AT&T 🛜 **Wi-Fi active**
High-Speed Data – Email, Web – OK
Phone / SMS Text = OK
Battery Life = Shorter
Download Smaller Apps - OK
Download Large Apps - OK

...ıll AT&T 3G **3G = 3G active**
High-Speed Data – Email, Web – OK
Phone / SMS Text = OK
Battery Life = Shorter
Download Smaller Apps - OK
Download Large Apps – Not available

...ıll AT&T E **E = EDGE active**
Low-Speed Data – Email, Web – OK
Phone / SMS Text = OK
Battery Life = Longer
Download Smaller Apps - OK
Download Large Apps – Not allowed

...ıll AT&T **(blank) = No data signal**
No data signal – Email, Web – Not available
Phone / SMS Text = OK
Battery Life = Longer
Download Smaller Apps – Not allowed
Download Large Apps – Not allowed

✈ **Airplane Mode**
No data signal – Email, Web – Not available
Phone / SMS Text = Not available
Battery Life = Longer
Download Smaller Apps – Not allowed
Download Large Apps – Not allowed

Why the network names change:
You will see the active network for your current location. For example, if you are in Canada, you will see the local **"ROGERS"** network instead of **"AT&T"** or some other network.

ROGERS Network (Canada)

..ıl.. ROGERS

Airplane Mode

When you are on an airplane: How to turn off the wireless radio (so it does not interfere with the airplane), but leave your iPhone on so you can listen to music, watch a video or play a game.

TIP: You know you are in Airplane Mode when you see the little airplane logo in the upper left corner as shown below.

Avoid High Unexpected Bills when Traveling (Data Roaming)

When you are traveling away from your home country, you will need to check with your wireless carrier (phone company) about how much data and voice roaming charges will be in your destination country or countries. If the charges are high or you don't know, then we highly recommend to **turn off Data Roaming** in your Settings Icon > General > Network as shown.

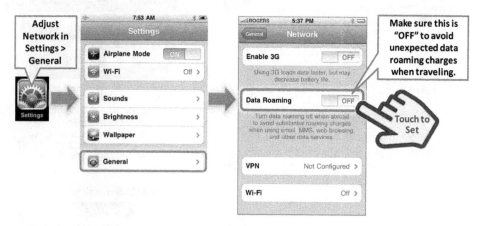

NOTE: If you are traveling, and WANT email, web, app downloads and other downloads to work, but are not worried about the data roaming charges, then you need to set "Data Roaming" to "ON."

Networks: High Speed ("3G") vs. Lower Speed 2G ("E") vs. Wi-Fi

Your iPhone can connect to the wireless cellular network with two data speeds and also to Wi-Fi or wireless local area networks. There are a few things you should keep in mind:

3G NETWORK: FASTEST CELLULAR NETWORK BUT "EATS" THE BATTERY

3G is faster than "E" or 2G networks, but consumes more battery life. So if you don't need a high speed data connection, then turn off 3G in Settings > General > Network. ("Enable 3G" to "OFF"). Another thing to be aware is that 3G coverage is usually limited to major metro areas and along major highways.

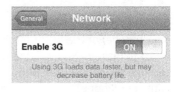

NO 3G SERVICE? TRY "E" (2G):

TRY THIS: Sometimes you will be in an area (usually rural) where there is no 3G network coverage, but there is "E" or 2G coverage. When you are in an area when you see "No Service" in the network status area (upper left corner of your home screen), try setting "Enable 3G" to "OFF." Sometimes this will allow you to get network connectivity, when you could not a signal at the 3G setting.

WI-FI NETWORKS: GREAT WHEN YOU ARE STATIONARY

Wi-Fi is faster than 3G, and is required to download larger apps (usually above 8 megabytes) from the App Store. However Wi-Fi is usually only available when you are stationary (e.g. at home, office, in a coffee shop or airport). However, be aware that Wi-Fi access away from your home or office may require you to purchase an extra service plan (e.g. Wi-Fi Hot Spot service plan). See page 196 for Wi-Fi help.

"E" or EDGE (2G): SAVES BATTERY WITH MINIMAL PERFORMANCE DROP

"E" or EDGE is the 2G or lower speed cellular data network and puts less strain on your iPhone battery. 2G still runs fairly fast and you may not notice the difference between 3G and 2G ("E") speeds. So in many cases you can disable 3G (Settings > General > Network - Set "Enable 3G" to "OFF"), to save your battery life without significant impact to your speed.

Your iPhone Touch Screen

The iPhone™ has an amazingly sensitive and intuitive touch screen. Apple®, renown for making computers and iPods easy to use, has come up with an excellent touch screen. And now, with version 3.0, the touch screen is even easier to type on with the larger keys on the 'landscape mode' keyboard (just hold your iPhone sideways).

If you are used to a physical keyboard and a trackball (dare we say a BlackBerry® Smartphone) or the iPod's intuitive scroll wheel, then this touch screen will take a little effort to master. You will find that with a little practice and patience as you work through this first section of the book you will soon become comfortable doing things with your iPhone™.

You can pretty much do anything on your iPhone™ by using a combination of:

- Touch screen 'gestures,'
- Touching any icon or soft key on the screen,
- Using the "Home" Button at the bottom.

Here is a summary of the basic touch screen gestures:

- **Touch** – To start an App Icon or confirm a selection, select a menu item, or select an answer simply touch the screen.

- **Swipe** – To move to the next picture in Photos or move through music library in "Cover Flow" view and to move between open Web pages – see page

- **Scroll up/down** – To scroll through Web Pages, Emails and Notes and more

- **Flick** – To move quickly through contacts, lists and music library in "list" mode. Flick side-to-side or up-and-down to scroll through items.

- **Double Tap** – **Zoom in / Zoom out** shortcut for a web page or Picture. Double-tap once to Zoom In and then again to Zoom Out again.

- **Open pinch** – **Zoom in**. When viewing a picture or web page, pinch your thumb and forefinger together then touch the screen and slide the fingers apart to zoom in.

- **Close Pinch - Zoom out** – When viewing a picture or web page, place two fingers (usually your thumb and forefinger) separated on the screen, then pinch them together while sliding them on the screen. This will zoom out (unless you are already zoomed out all the way).

Basic Touch Screen Gestures

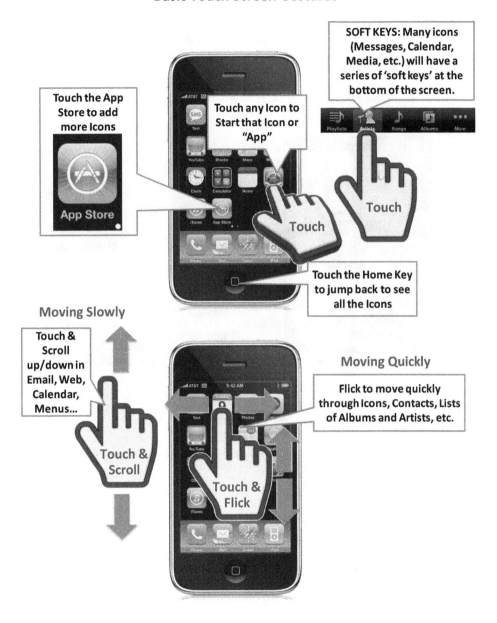

SOFT KEYS: Many icons (Messages, Calendar, Media, etc.) will have a series of 'soft keys' at the bottom of the screen.

Touch the App Store to add more Icons

Touch any Icon to Start that Icon or "App"

Touch

Touch

Touch the Home Key to jump back to see all the Icons

Moving Slowly

Touch & Scroll up/down in Email, Web, Calendar, Menus...

Touch & Scroll

Moving Quickly

Flick to move quickly through Icons, Contacts, Lists of Albums and Artists, etc.

Touch & Flick

Starting Icons & Using Soft Keys

Simply touch any icon to start it.

Inside most icons, you will see soft keys at the bottom to perform common tasks.
In the Music icon, the soft keys allow you to quickly switch between different popular views of your music: Playlists, Artists, Songs, and Albums.

TIP: You know which soft key is selected because it is highlighted - usually with a color - the other soft keys are usually gray in color but still can be touched.

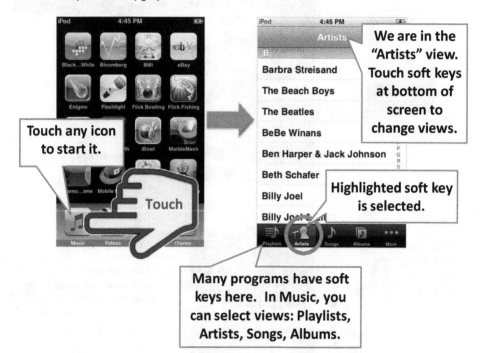

Touch any icon to start it.

Touch

We are in the "Artists" view. Touch soft keys at bottom of screen to change views.

Highlighted soft key is selected.

Many programs have soft keys here. In Music, you can select views: Playlists, Artists, Songs, Albums.

Menus, Sub-Menus and Switches

Simply touch any menu item to select it.

MENUS AND SUB-MENUS:
Level of menu below the main level. TIP: You know there is a sub-menu or another screen if you see the greater than symbol next to the menu item ("**>**").

How to get into a SUB-MENU?
Just tap on the menu name. (Like "General" below in the Settings menu)

How to get back up to the previous menu?
Just tap the name of the previous menu at the top left of the menu title bar. Like "Settings" in the General menu below.

SETTING SWITCHES:
You will see switches like the ON / OFF switch next to "Location Services" below. To set a switch (e.g. from ON to OFF), just touch it.

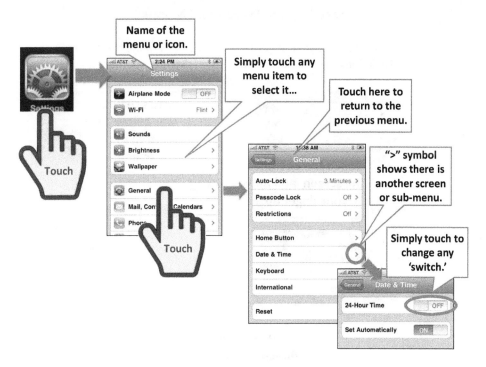

Swipe – Quickly Move between Web Pages, Pictures and In Lists

Gently touch and swipe or flick your finger. Move between open Web Pages and Pictures.   Also works in lists like your Contacts list.

Scrolling the Screen and Menus

Simply tap and slide your finger to move or scroll around the screen.
Use in Messages (Email), Web Browser, Menus and more…

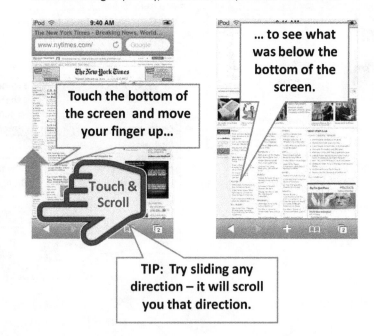

Tap the Screen to Show / Hide Controls or Soft Keys

When playing a song or video, just tap anywhere in the middle of the screen to show or hide the controls at the top of the screen.

Double Tap to Quickly Zoom In or Out
(Works on Web Pages, Email Messages, and Pictures)

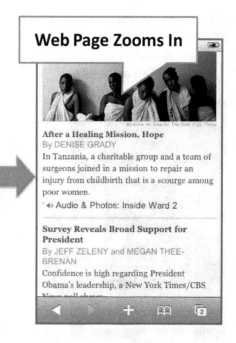

"Pinch" Open or Closed to Gradually Zoom Out or In
(Works on Web Pages, Email Messages, and Pictures)

ZOOM IN:
In Pictures and Web Pages, touch the screen with 2 fingers and Pinch Open.

Think: *"I'm making this portion of the picture bigger"*

Pinch Open

Zoom in on the 'pinched' section

Pinch Open

Picture Zooms In Even More...

ZOOM OUT:
Touch the screen with 2 fingers apart and Pinch Closed.

Think: *"I'm shrinking this portion of the picture"*

Pinch Closed

Zoom Out on the 'pinched' section

Pinch Closed

Picture Zooms Out Even More...

Touch and Hold to Activate "Magnifying Glass" to Place Cursor

Need to correct a typing error in the middle of a word or sentence?

Touch and hold to see the Magnifying Glass, to easily position the cursor.

...Then tap the end of the text to position the cursor at the end of the text.

Type any letter or hit the backspace key to make your corrections at the cursor...

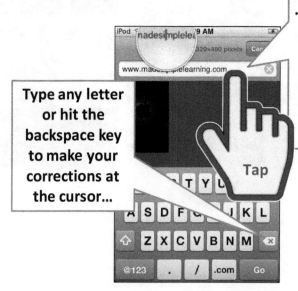

Introduction

Congratulations on your iPhone!

In your hands is perhaps the most powerful and elegant Smartphone available today – the iPhone.

The "Original" iPod was a breakthrough Media Player. Apple has taken all the features of its popular iPod Touch and packaged them in this powerful device that is a fully functioning phone and much more.

You can not only manage all your Media – pictures, music and videos – but also keep your schedule, find things with a powerful mapping App, keep track of your contacts, email, go online and download any one of thousands of fantastic Games and Apps from the "App Store" and more.

Things this powerful are not always easy to grasp – at first

You will soon realize that your iPhone is a very powerful device. There are, however, many secrets "locked" inside that we help you "unlock" throughout this book.

Anyone new to a touch screen on a phone may not see the Apple "intuitive" design at first glance. This new touch screen might even be frustrating – you want your iPhone to do what your old phone with the physical keypad did – in just the same way!

Take your time – this book can help you on your way to learning how to best use and work with your new iPhone. Think back to when you tried to use your first Windows™ or Mac™ computer? It took a little while to get familiar with how to do things. It's the same with the iPhone. Use this book to help you get up to speed and learn all the best tips and tricks more quickly.

Why do I see both iPod Touch and iPhone Screens?

Wherever the functionality is identical between the iPod Touch and the iPhone, we do use some iPod Touch screens in this book. Don't worry if you see the little "iPod" in the upper left corner.

BONUS: This means most of what you learn in this iPhone book will also help you learn how to use and master an iPod Touch.

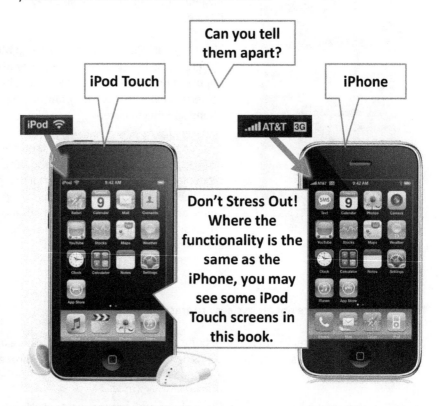

The only difference between the two will be in the upper left hand corner the words iPod may appear instead of the bars of service strength and the Wireless Carrier name.

Day in the Life of an iPhone User

Sometimes it's easier to learn by watching someone use their iPhone. The next best thing is to read about it. With this section, we try to help you begin to understand how you might best use your iPhone in your own work and personal life.

Time	What I do with my iPhone...	Learn more...
6:00 AM	My iPhone Alarm wakes me.	Page 308
6:10 AM	I plug my iPhone into my docking station in the bathroom to listen to my music, my favorite podcast or NPR.	Play Music - iPod - p. 169 iTunes - p. 320
6:45 AM	At the breakfast table, I check my email, browse the New York Times articles from my NY Times Icon (from the App Store).	Page 338
6:55 AM	I check traffic using Google Maps and find out I need to take my alternate route to work today.	Page 285
7:00 AM	I pair up my iPhone with my Stereo Bluetooth in the car to listen to a lecture from Boston University on the way to work.	Page 137
8:30 AM	Waiting for a meeting, I read and respond to email.	Page 216
10:00 AM	I find out I have to fly to Los Angeles tonight to visit a client - so I check travel web sites on my iPhone and book my airplane and rental car.	Page 203
10:05 AM	I received an email message from my client with the location of our meeting in L.A. so I mapped the address and then added this as a new Contact entry for easy access during my trip.	Copy/Paste - page 55 Maps - page 288
10:10 AM	I need to find hotels around my Client's address so I just type 'hotels' into Maps search window and quickly find all hotels in the area.	Maps - page 288
10:15 AM	Armed with some hotel options, I book my hotel, flight and rental car using either Safari or my Travel App.	Page 203
10:25 AM	I add Los Angeles to my Weather icon and	Page 316

	see that it will be really hot. Now I know how I need to pack.	
11:00 AM	I receive an SMS from my spouse - "Want to have lunch at Spagos at 1:15 today?"	Page 145
11:05 AM	I lookup Spago's phone number and call them using Maps to reserve a table.	Maps - page 288
11:07 AM	I reply to the SMS message and say "Sure - we're all set for 1PM - see you there!"	Page 145
1:30 PM	I show my spouse my cool new pictures I took on the iPhone in the Photos Icon.	Page 269
2:30 PM	I take pictures of my new client's art work with my iPhone to send to a prospective buyer. I select and email 5 great snapshots of the best work.	Camera - Page 131 Email Pictures - Page 274
3:45 PM	The buyer emails me back and says she wants to buy some of the art pieces. I click on her phone number in her email signature and give her a call right away. I then conference call the artist and we seal the deal right there.	Page 106
4:30 PM	Another check of Google Maps for traffic for the commute home to pack, and again for the trip to the airport. Armed with the latest information, I'm set.	Page 285
8:00 PM	Sitting at the gate in the airport, I browse the iTunes store on my iPhone and decide to rent and download a movie. I enable Wi-Fi for a faster download.	iTunes on iPhone - p. 320 Wi-Fi - p. 196
8:50 PM	I settle into my seat and make sure to turn on Airplane Mode so I can use my iPhone without causing trouble with the pilots.	Airplane Mode - p. 20
9:00 PM	Sitting back in my seat, I plug in my headset and watch my newly rented movie on the flight to Los Angeles. Another great day with my iPhone!	Watch movies - p. 188

Chapter 1:
Learning your Way Around

IMPORTANT! Before You Read Any Further!

Before you do anything with your new iPhone, please take a few minutes to check out our "**Quick Reference Guide**" pages earlier in this book. They are meant to help you find lots of useful things in this book as well as some great beginner and advanced time-saving tips and tricks to get up and running quickly.

Protecting Your iPhone

Once you have your iPhone in your hands you will notice how beautifully it is constructed. You will also notice that it is fairly slippery. There are many user stories of iPhone being dropped, scratched or literally sliding out of a person's hand - so we recommend buying a protective case.   Average cases run about US$ 10 - 25 and "fancy" leather cases can run upwards of US$ 100. Spending a little to protect your iPhone that cost several hundred dollars makes good sense.

Where to buy:
Amazon.com (http://www.amazon.com)
The iPhone Blog Store (http://store.theiphoneblog.com/)
The Apple Accessory Store: (http://store.apple.com)
iLounge: (http://ilounge.pricegrabber.com)
You could also do a web search for "iphone cases"

Rubber / Silicone Cases ($10 - $30)
What these do: Provide a cushioned grip and should absorb iPhone bumps and bruises
Pros: Inexpensive, colorful and comfortable to hold
Cons: Not as "professional" as a leather case

Hard Plastic / Metal Case ($15 - $40)
> **What these do:** Provide hard, solid protection against scratches and bumps and short drops.
> **Pros**: Provides good protection
> **Cons**: Adds some bulk and weight

Leather "Book" or "Flip" Cases ($20 - $100)
> **What these do:** Provide more of a "luxury" feel- protect the front and sides as well as the back.
> **Pros**: Leather "luxury" feel, protects the front and the back
> **Cons**: More expensive, adds bulk and weight

Screen Protectors ($4 - $25)
> **What these do:** Protect the screen from scratches
> **Pros**: Help prolong life of phone, protect against scratches
> **Cons**: Some can increase glare, may affect "touch" sensitivity of the screen

Powering On and Off and Sleep Mode

To turn on your iPhone, press and hold the power key on the top right edge of the iPhone for a few seconds. Simply tapping this button quickly won't power on the phone if it is completely off -- you really need to hold it until you see the iPhone power on.

When you are no longer using your iPhone you have two options: you can either put it into "sleep" mode or turn it off completely.

The advantage of "Sleep Mode" is that when you want to use your iPhone again, just a quick tap of the "On/Off" button or pressing the "Home" button will bring your iPhone back awake. This convenience comes at the price of battery life.

If you want to maximize your battery or if you know you won't be using your iPhone for quite some time - say when you go to sleep - you might want to turn it off completely. The way to do this is to press and hold the "On/Off" button until you see the "Slide to Power Off" bar appear. Just slide the bar to the right and the iPhone will power off.

**On/Off &
Wake/Sleep Button**

Tap quickly to put
into Sleep Mode
Or...

Press & Hold about 4
seconds until you see
"Slide to power off"
on your screen.
Then, slide your
finger to power off
your iPhone.

Airplane Mode

When you are traveling on an airplane, be sure to enable 'Airplane Mode' by going into the Settings Icon and tapping the "ON" button next to Airplane Mode a the top. This turns off your wireless radio signal and allows you to continue using your iPhone for music, videos, games, calendar and more, but not interfere with the pilots. You know Airplane mode is turned on when you

see a little airplane icon ✈ in the upper right corner, where you used to see your signal strength letters and wireless network name.

The "Home" Button

The key to beginning to use your iPhone is locating and pressing the "Home" button. This button will begin everything you do with your iPhone. Press it once to "Wake up" your iPhone (assuming it is in Sleep mode.)

If your iPhone is completely "Turned Off," just press and hold the On/Off button located on the top of the iPhone. The Home key is the button you will use most on your iPhone. Pressing the Home button will wake your iPhone if it is sleeping. Pressing the Home button will take you out of any program you are in and bring you back to your Home screen.

TIP: Double-tapping your Home Button can be set to do different things like starting the iPod function, Phone Favorites, or more. (See how to configure this on page 40).

Learning When Email, Web and App Downloads Work

Check out the Quick Reference chart on page 19 to show you how to check the letters and symbols in the upper left corner of your iPhone so you know exactly when email, web browsing, app download and more are working.

TIP: If your data connectivity is not working well, then try turning Airplane Mode on and off. That sometimes helps. It that does not help, then try turning your iPhone off then on. Finally, if you need more help then try out some of the troubleshooting tips found on page 355.

Sleep/Wake Button (And Power Button)

The Power button doubles as the Sleep / Wake Up Button.

You can also use a short press of this button to put your iPhone into "Sleep" mode or to "Wake" it up when it is 'sleeping.'

The Mute / Ringer Off and Volume Keys

MUTE / RINGER OFF KEY

Handy when going into that movie, meal or meeting... this switch will turn off the ringer on the iPhone and set it to vibrate when calls or messages come in by sliding it to the back of the iPhone. You know you have turned MUTE on when you feel a brief vibration and see a bell with a line through it on the screen. Also, you will see that an orange dot is visible next to the switch.

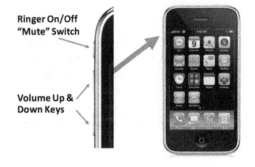

Ringer On/Off "Mute" Switch

Volume Up & Down Keys

VOLUME KEYS

Located on the left-hand side of the iPhone, these are simple Volume up/volume down keys that you will find very handy. In many places, you can also control the volume of the song, video or podcast playing by sliding your finger on the screen volume control.

Double-Clicking The "Home" Key

You can customize what happens when you double-click (or double-tap) the Home Key.

In order to Just touch the "**Settings**" icon and touch the "**General**" tab. Scroll down, and you will see that there is a tab labeled "**Home Button.**"

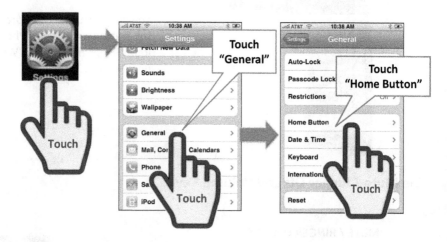

After you touch the "Home Button," you will see several options under "**Double-clicking the Home Button goes to:**"

Just tap the selection you want for the Home button.

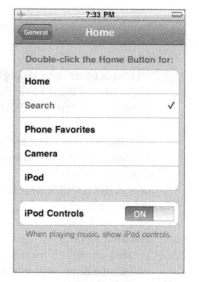

Home:
This is essentially the same thing as pressing the "Home Button" once.

Search:
Will bring up the Search icon to find anything on your iPhone in Contacts, Music, Email, Calendar and more.

Phone Favorites:
If you select this option, whenever you double-click the "Home Button" you will immediately bring up your "**Phone Favorites**" discussed on Page 106. This allows you to easily call one of your favorites from any application.

Camera:
Select this option to bring up the Camera when you double-click "Home."
Learn more about the Camera on page 131.

iPod:
Select this to bring up the iPod when you double-click the "Home" button.
When you double-click "Home" while playing music (and your "iPod Controls"
is set to "ON") you will see the iPod controls appear.
If iPod Controls is set to "OFF" then double-clicking "Home" will automatically
bring you into the iPod, whether or not you are listening to music. This is
very helpful is you are in the midst of listening to music and want to quickly
pause or change the song.

Slide to Unlock

When you first power on your iPhone, you will see the "Slide to Unlock"
screen. Just follow the path of the arrow and gently "Slide" the unlock button
to the right.

Once you do that, you will see your Home Screen.

BOTTOM DOCK: You will see four icons "locked" in the Bottom Dock while
the rest of the icons can move back and forth in 'pages' above this Bottom
Dock. Learn how to move your favorite icons into the Bottom Dock in our
"Moving Icons" section on page 157.

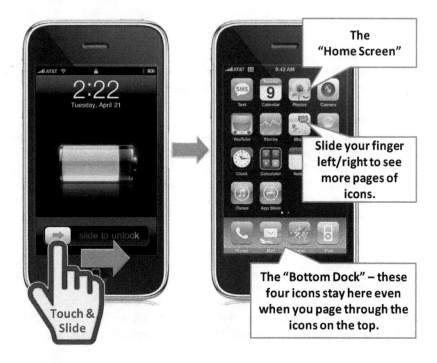

The "Home Screen"

Slide your finger left/right to see more pages of icons.

The "Bottom Dock" – these four icons stay here even when you page through the icons on the top.

Touch & Slide

To Adjust or Disable the "Auto Lock" Feature

After you have your iPhone for just a little while, you will notice that it will "Auto Lock" and go into "Sleep Mode" with the screen blank after a short amount of time. You can change this time or even disable this feature altogether inside the Settings Icon.

Touch the "Settings" icon on the Home Screen. Touch the "General" tab and scroll down to "Auto Lock."

The default setting is that the iPhone locks after one minute of sitting idle (to save battery life.) You can change this to 2, 3, 4, 5 minutes or **Never**.

Touch the desired setting to select it - you know it's selected when you see the checkmark next to it (like **2 minutes** in the image).

Then, touch the "**General**" tab in the upper left hand corner to get back to the "**General Screen**." You should see your change now reflected next to "**Auto Lock**."

BATTERY LIFE TIP:
Setting the Auto-Lock shorter (e.g. 1 minute) will help you save battery life.

Adjusting the Date and Time

Usually, the date and time are adjusted automatically using the wireless phone network or when you connect your iPhone to your computer (which we cover in the next chapter). You can also manually adjust your date and time in the Settings Icon. Touch the Settings Icon, then touch "**General**," and finally "**Date & Time**" to see the Date & Time settings screen.

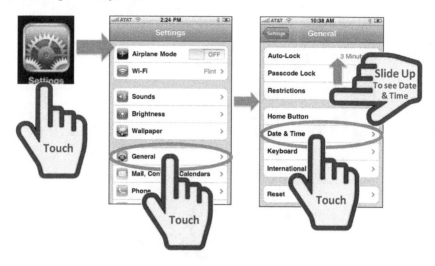

24-Hour Time

If you prefer to see 09:30 and 14:30 instead of 9:30 AM and 2:30 PM, then you will want to turn ON the "**24-Hour Time**" setting by tapping the switch to slide it to "**ON**."

Set Automatically = ON

The default is "**ON**" for this setting which will have your date, time, time-zone and daylight savings time be adjusted automatically from the time from the wireless (cell phone) network.

Set Automatically = OFF

If you have the "**Set Automatically**" set to "**OFF**," you will then see the options for setting the Time Zone and the Date and time.

SETTING YOUR TIME ZONE

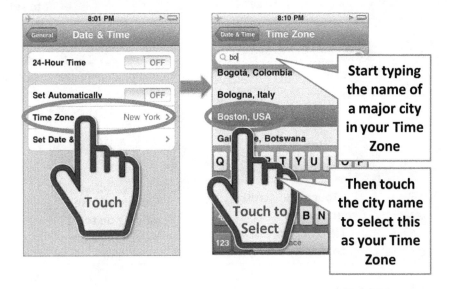

To set the time zone, touch the "**Time Zone**" tab and start to type in the name of the desired city. Touch the Bold print for the city and the screen will automatically move back to the "**Date and Time**" screen you were in before.

SETTING YOUR DATE & TIME

To set the "**Date and Time**" touch the "**Set Date and Time**" tab and you will see three individual "wheels" that rotate as you touch and move them.

So, in the example below, we touch and slide the hour "Wheel" and to move it upwards to change the time from 10 to 11.

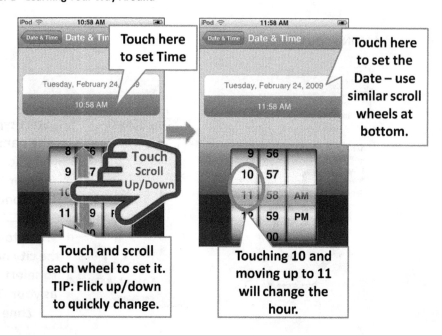

Adjusting the Brightness

From your Home screen, once again touch the "**Settings**" icon. The "**Brightness**" tab is in the middle of the screen. Touch the Brightness tab and then move the slider control to adjust the brightness.

Your iPhone has an "Auto-Brightness" control available, which is usually the default. This uses the built in light sensor to adjust the brightness of the screen. Generally, we advise that you keep this set to "**ON**."

BATTERY LIFE TIP:
Setting the brightness lower will help you save battery life. A little less than 1/2 way across seems to work fine.

Chapter 2:
Typing Tips, Copy/Paste & Search

In this chapter, we show you how to best type on your iPhone, whether you use the portrait (vertical/smaller) keyboard or landscape (horizontal/larger) keyboard (requires 3.0 software). You will also learn how to select different language keyboards, how to type symbols and other tips.

Also learn about the spotlight search and the Copy and Paste function - new with 3.0 software, that will save you lots of time as well as increase accuracy with your iPhone.

Basic Typing Tips - One Finger vs. Two Thumbs

You will find when you first start out with your iPhone, you can more easily type with one finger - usually your index finger - while holding the iPhone with the other.

After a little while, you should be able to experiment with 'thumb typing' (like you see so many people doing with their BlackBerry smartphones). Typing with two thumbs instead of a single finger, once you get used to it, will really boost your speed. Just be patient, it does take a little practice to become proficient typing quickly with your two thumbs.

You will actually notice after a while that the keyboard touch sensitivity assumes you are typing with two thumbs. What this means is that the letters on the left side of your keyboard are meant to be pressed on their left side, and the right side keys are meant to be touched/pressed on their right side.

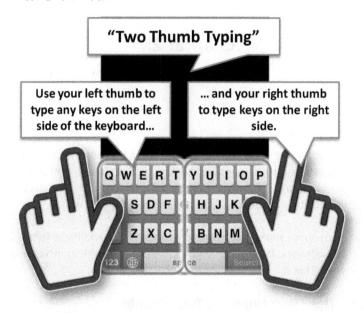

TIP: If you have larger hands, (and you have installed 3.0 software), then flip your iPhone on its side to get the larger, landscape keyboard (see below).

Landscape Larger Keyboard

Before 3.0 software, you could only get a larger "Landscape" keyboard in the Safari Web Browser, but not anywhere else. Now, with 3.0, you can flip your iPhone on its side to use the larger, roomier "Landscape" keyboard when typing.

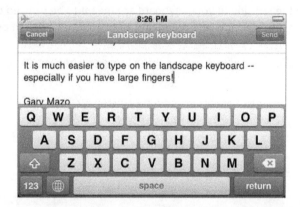

Just turn the iPhone sideways in almost any application icon and the keyboard will change to a larger, landscape "QWERTY" keyboard for typing.

Saving Time with Auto-Correction (Pop-Up Guessed Words)

When you are typing for a while, you will begin to notice a little pop-up window directly below some of the words you are typing -- this is called "Auto-Correction." (If you never see this pop-up window, then you will have to enable Auto-Correction in your Settings Icon - see page 54.) You can save yourself time when you see the correct word guessed, just press the 'space' key at the bottom of the keyboard to select that word.

In this example we start typing the word 'especially,' and when we get to the 'c' in the word, the correct word 'especially' appears below in a pop-up. To select it, we simply press the 'space' key at the bottom.

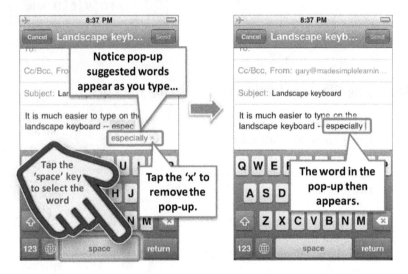

Your first inclination might be to tap the pop-up word, but that simply erases it from the screen. (This might be one of the very few seemingly counter-intuitive things you can find on the iPhone.) After you learn to use the 'space' key, you will see that this pop-up guessing can be quite a time saver. After all, you were going to have to type a space at the end of the word anyways!

TIME SAVING TIP: With Auto-Correction, you can save time by skipping typing the apostrophe in many common contractions like "wont" and "cant." Auto-Correction will show you a little pop-up window with the contraction spelled correctly, all you need to do to select the correction is to press the SPACE key.

Magnifying Glass for Editing Text / Placing the Cursor

How many times have you been typing something and wanted to move the cursor precisely between two words, or between two letters?

This can be hard to do until you figure out the "Magnifying Glass" trick. What you do is this: touch and hold your finger on the place where you want the cursor. After a second or two, you will see the magnifying glass appear. Then, while you hold your finger on the screen, slide it around to position the cursor. It is much easier!

Tap and hold to see the magnifying glass... slide your finger to place the cursor.

Typing Numbers and Symbols

How do you type a number or a symbol on the iPhone? When you are typing, tap the '123' key in the lower left corner to see numbers and common symbols like '$! ~ & = # . _ - +.' If you need more symbols, then from the number keyboard, tap the '#+=' key just above the ABC key in the lower left corner.

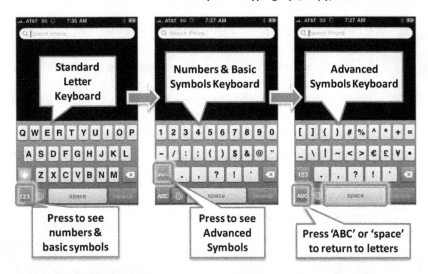

Standard Letter Keyboard

Numbers & Basic Symbols Keyboard

Advanced Symbols Keyboard

Press to see numbers & basic symbols

Press to see Advanced Symbols

Press 'ABC' or 'space' to return to letters

TIP: Notice that the number or symbol keyboard will stay active until you either hit the 'space' key or tap the key for another keyboard like 'ABC.'

What about symbols not shown on the keyboard?

TIP: You can type more symbols than are shown on the screen.

All you do is press and hold a letter, number or symbol that is related to the symbol you want.

For example, if you wanted to type the EURO symbol (€), you would press and hold the $ key until you saw the other options, then slide up your finger to highlight and then let go on the EURO symbol.

Tap and hold to see the pop-up... then slide your finger to type one of the characters.

Tap and hold until you see the pop-up

TIP: There is a good bullet point character on the Advanced Symbols screen right above the backspace key.

Typing In Other Languages - International Keyboards

At publishing time, the iPhone allowed you to enable to type in over 40 different languages including languages from Arabic to Ukrainian. Some of the Asian languages such as Japanese and Chinese offer 2 or 3 keyboards for different forms of input.

To enable various language keyboards, touch the "Settings" Icon, then tap "General." From here, you can get into the Keyboard Language list two ways: Tap "International," then tap "Keyboards" or from General, tap "Keyboards," then "International Keyboards." To enable any language keyboard, simply tap the "OFF" to change it to an "ON."

Once you have enabled a number of keyboards, then you tap the Globe key to cycle between all the languages.

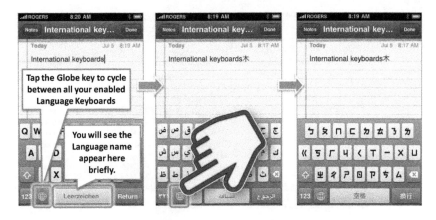

Some of the languages, like Japanese have several keyboard options to meet your typing preferences.

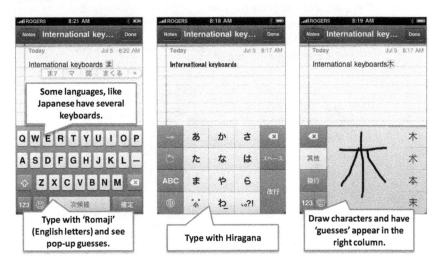

In some of the languages, (such as Japanese shown below) you will see the Auto-Correction pop-up window appear below the line you are typing. This will show you some popular options or, sometimes give you an arrow to see a window of many more options. Tap the right-arrow to see these options, then scroll up or down to view everything. Finally, tap to select a character or set of characters.

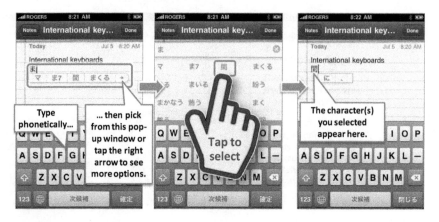

Keyboard Options & Settings

There are a few options for your Keyboard – to make typing easier – on your iPhone. The keyboard options are located in the "**General**" tab of your "Settings."

Touch the "**Settings**" icon, then "General" and then scroll down and touch **Keyboard**.

Auto-Correction ON / OFF

Using the built in dictionary, Auto-Correction will automatically make changes in commonly misspelled words. For example, if you type in wont, Auto Correction will change it to "won't" on the fly. You need to make sure it is "ON" if you want this feature to work. (This is the default setting.)

Auto-Capitalization

When you start a new sentence, words will automatically be capitalized if Auto-Capitalization is "ON."

Also, common proper nouns will be correctly capitalized. For example if you typed "New york," you would be prompted to change it to "New York" - again just pressing the SPACE key will select the correction.

This is also set to "ON" by default.

Enable Caps Lock

Sometimes when you type, you may want to "Lock" the Caps – just like you do on a computer keyboard. "Enabling" Caps Lock will allow you to do this. Again, this is set to "ON" by default.

"." Shortcut

If you are a BlackBerry user, you might be familiar with the feature that will automatically put in a "period" at the end of the sentence when you double tap the "Space" key. This is exactly the same feature that you can enable on the iPhone. By default, this is also set to "ON."

Copy and Paste

Perhaps no feature was more widely requested by iPhone users than "Cut and Paste." Now, in version 3.0, you have the ability to select text from a web site, an email, a note – virtually anywhere on your iPhone and then copy it into any other App where you can input text.

"Copy and Paste" is very useful for taking text from your calendar and putting it in an Email or taking a note and placing it in an Email or in your Calendar – there are lots of applications for "Copy and Paste." You can even copy text from your Safari web browser and paste it into a Note or a Mail message.

Selecting Text with Double-tap

If you are reading or typing text, you can double-tap to start selecting text for the copy. This works well in "Mail," "Messages" (SMS Text), "Notes" You will see a box with blue dots ("handles") at opposite corners. Just drag the handles to select the text you with to highlight and "copy."

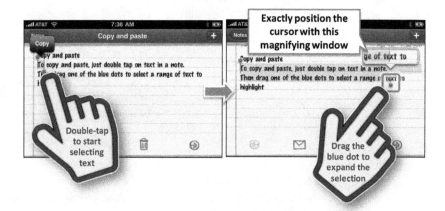

TIP: If you want to select all the text, then double-tap the screen above or below the text. Then you should see a pop-up showing you "Select" or "Select All." Tap "Select All" to highlight all the text.

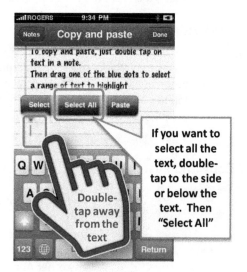

Selecting Text with "Two Finger Touch"

The other way to select text requires that you touch the screen simultaneously with two fingers. This seems to work best if you are holding your iPhone with one hand and use your thumb and forefinger from your other hand to touch the screen. What you want to do is touch the screen at the beginning and end of the text you want to select. Don't worry if you cannot get the selection exactly correct the first touch. Just use the blue handles to drag the selection to the correct position.

Selecting Text with "Touch and Hold"

In the Safari web browser, hold your finger on some text and the paragraph will become highlighted with "Handles" at each of the corners.

Drag the handles if you want to select even more text.

Cut or Copy the Text

Once you have the text highlighted that you wish to copy, just touch the "Copy" tab at the top of the screen. The tab will turn "Blue" indicating that the text is on the clipboard.

NOTE: If you have previously "Cut" or "Copied" text, then you will also see the "Paste" option as shown.

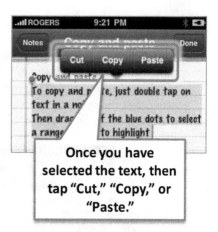

Once you have selected the text, then tap "Cut," "Copy," or "Paste."

To "Paste" the Text

If you are pasting the text into the same note or mail message:

If you are pasting the text in the same note or mail message in which you copied the text, then you need to move the cursor to where you want to paste the text. Remember the 'Magnifying Glass' trick (page 30) to help you position the cursor. Once you let go, you should see a pop-up asking you to "Select," "Select All," or "Paste." If you don't see this pop-up, then double-tap the screen.

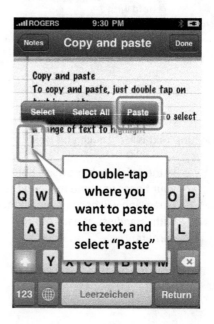

Double-tap where you want to paste the text, and select "Paste"

If you want to paste the text into another Icon:

Press the "Home" button and tap the icon into which you want to paste the text. Let's say we wanted to paste the text into a Mail message. Then we would tap the "Mail" icon and compose a new message. Then double-tap anywhere in the body of the message and select "Paste."

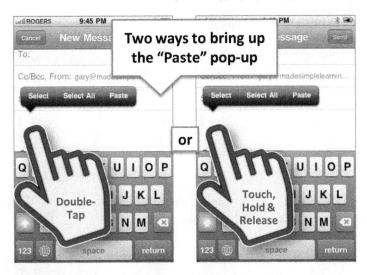

Move the cursor to the body of the text and either double-tap or touch, hold and release your finger in and you will see the "Paste" pop-up. Tap "Paste" and the text on the clipboard will be pasted right into the body of the email.

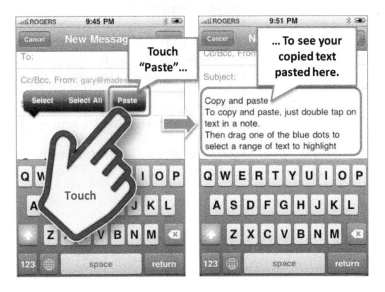

"Shake" to Undo Paste or Typing

One of the great new features in "Copy and Paste" is the ability to undo either typing or the "Paste" you just completed.

All you have to do is "Shake" the iPhone after the paste. A new pop-up appears giving you the option to "undo" what you have just done.

Select "**Undo Paste**" and or "**Undo Typing**" to correct the mistake.

Finding Things with "Spotlight Search"

New in version 3.0 is "**Spotlight Search**" - Apple's proprietary search method for a global search through your iPhone for a name, event or subject. The concept is simple; let's say we am looking for something related to Martin. We cannot remember if it was an Email, a Note, or a Calendar event, but we do know it was related to Martin.

This is the perfect time to use the "Spotlight Search" feature to find everything related to "Martin" on my iPhone.

Activating "Spotlight Search"

First, we need to get into the Spotlight Search which resides to the left of the first page of the Home Screen.

On the left side of the first circle (indicating the first page of your Home Screen) is a very small magnifying glass.

Swipe to the right of this first page of icons to get to the "Spotlight Search" page.

On the Search page, type in one or a few words for your search.

TIP: If you are looking for a person, then type their full name to more accurately find items from only that person. (E.g. "Martin Trautschold") This will eliminate any other "Martins" who might be in my iPhone and make sure we find items only related to "Martin Trautschold."

In the search result, we see all emails, appointments, meeting invitations and contact information appears. Tap one of the results in the list to view its contents.

Your search results stay there until you clear them, so you can go back to "Spotlight Search" once again by swiping to the right from your Home Screen.

To clear the search field, just touch the "X" in the search bar. To exit "Spotlight Search," just press the "Home" key or swipe to the left.

Chapter 3:
iTunes - Sync with Computer,
Buy Music & More

Whether you work on a PC or a Mac, the software you use on your computer is the same: iTunes.

What can iTunes do for you and your iPhone?

- Transfer or "synchronize" your Music, Pictures and Video collection
- Transfer or "synchronize" your personal information (addresses, calendar, notes) between your computer and your iPhone
- Backup and restore your iPhone data
- Install or remove application icons (those that you do not install using the App Store on the phone).

What if I already use an iPod?

You may have a few of these questions:
Can I put all my purchased music on my iPhone? Yes! You will tie your iPhone to iTunes on your computer as your own device, so you can put all your purchased music right on your iPhone - no problem.

Can I keep using my iPod? Yes! You can definitely keep listening to all your music on both your iPod and your new iPhone.

Can I use my same iTunes software and account from before? Yes! This is fine - you can use the same iTunes software already installed on your computer and your same iTunes account to setup your iPhone.

Other questions you may have about connecting your iPhone to your computer:

What if I use Microsoft(r) Outlook(tm) or another software to manage my email, contacts and calendar?
Configure iTunes to "Synchronize" your Data   Page 97

What if I use Google for my email, my contacts and possibly my calendar?
Enable "Google Sync" on page 92

What if I use Yahoo for my email and contacts?
If you have "Outlook" or "iCal" subscribe to your Yahoo Calendar, it will appear as a calendar you can choose to Sync – see Page 92

What if I have an existing cell phone that I want to transfer the contacts (and other information) to my iPhone?
First, transfer the information to Outlook (if you are a Windows user,) or iCal or Entourage (if you are a Mac User) or Google Calendar and Contacts. Then, follow the directions above.

If you have iTunes Installed Already, Check Your Current Version

If you have already installed iTunes, you should check which version you currently have. The easiest was to do that is start up your iTunes program, go to "Help" (on your PC) or iTunes (farthest menu to the left on the Mac) and then to "About iTunes." You will see right here that the version number of your particular version is shown. If you don't have version 8.2 or higher – it is time to upgrade.

Download iTunes from the Apple Web site

If you decide you need to download and install the latest version of iTunes, go to www.itunes.com/download. This link works equally well for both PC and Mac users and download and install the latest version of the software.

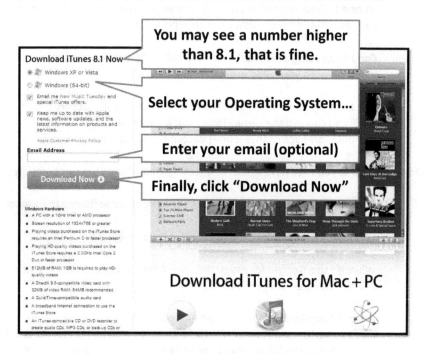

Overview of iTunes and Free Tutorials from Apple

iTunes is designed to help you manage your media and to configure to sync with your iPhone. In iTunes, you can arrange your music, create playlists, manage Video files and podcasts and more.

In iTunes, you can also configure your iPhone to sync with your personal information, data and pictures, as we will explain later in this chapter. It is a good idea to familiarize yourself with the features of iTunes by going to http://www.apple.com/itunes/tutorials/ and watching the various iTunes tutorials.

OUR VIDEO TUTORIALS: Made Simple Learning has produced over 400 short 3-minute video tutorials for the BlackBerry(r) Smartphones and are exploring making similar videos for the iPhone and iPod Touch. Please visit our site http://www.madesimplelearning.com/index.shtml to see if we have some videos available by the time you read this book.

On a Windows PC, after you download the **iTunesSetup.exe** file and double click on it to start it, you may see a warning similar to the one shown. Just click on "Run" to start the setup.

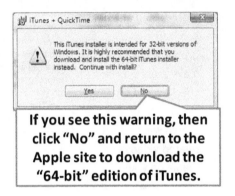

If you see a 64-bit warning message similar to this one, then please click "No" and return to the Apple site to download the 64-bit edition of iTunes better suited for your computer.
www.itunes.com/download

Next, follow the on-screen instructions to complete the installation of iTunes on your computer.

Running iTunes the First Time - the "Setup Assistant"

If you are just running iTunes for the first time on your computer, you will be asked a few questions by the "iTunes Setup Assistant" to help iTunes work better for you.

The screens below show a Windows computer version of iTunes, but the process is very similar on a Mac computer.

Click the "Next" button to get started.

> **Click "Next" to start the iTunes Setup Assistant**

If you have other media (songs, videos, etc.) on your computer, you probably want to leave these boxes checked and click "Next." Note: This search will find ALL related videos and media on your computer and could take quite a while!

> **If you leave these two boxes checked, then all available (unprotected) music on your computer will be added to your iTunes library.**

We recommend leaving the default "No."

WARNING: Choosing "Yes" will cause videos, music and other media in separate directories to be moved out of these directories into the iTunes directory causing other programs that

> **"Yes" = You want iTunes to re-organize your music on your computer (rename, change folders)**
> **"No" (default) = Leave all music alone on your computer.**

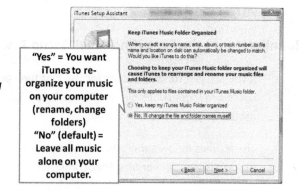

access this media to no longer function correctly!

On this final screen, it just explains that iTunes will attempt to download album art (the cover of the Album/CD). You can manually get album art in iTunes, we show you how on page 72.

Click "Finish."

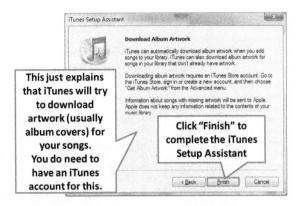

This just explains that iTunes will try to download artwork (usually album covers) for your songs. You do need to have an iTunes account for this.

Click "Finish" to complete the iTunes Setup Assistant

Now you will see a search status screen attempting to find all media compatible with iTunes (videos, music and more).

If you asked iTunes to search for media (songs & videos), then you will see this "Adding Files" status window until iTunes finds all your media.

Also, you may notice at the top of your iTunes screen that it is busy converting some of your media into a format compatible with iTunes and your iPhone (usually called "AAC").

During this conversion process, you will also see the main iTunes window with "Converting" for all music that is not in AAC format. Depending on the number of songs that need to be converted, this could take a long time.

iTunes Basics - Playing Songs, Videos and More

If you are new to iTunes, there are a few basic pointers on how to get around.

Playing a Song or Video: Just double click on it to start playing it.

Controlling the Song or Video: Use the Rewind, Pause, Fast-Forward Buttons and Volume Slider in the upper left corner to control the playback.

Moving to a different part of the Song or Video: Just click on the diamond in slider bar under the song name in the top of the window and drag it left or right as desired.

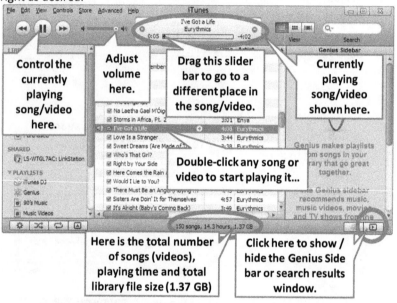

iTunes Basics - Creating a New Playlist

You may be used to listening to all the music on a particular Album, but you will soon find the benefits of creating your own custom Playlists. These are lists of particular songs that you group together.

Playlists could be any grouping you like for example:
- Workout Music
- Favorite U2 Songs
- Traveling Music

To create a new playlist, you can press "**Ctrl + N**" (or **Command + N** on a Mac,) select "**New Playlist**" from the "**File**" menu, or simply click the **New Playlist button** in the lower left corner of iTunes, as shown.

Then type the name of your playlist.

NOTE: On a Mac, it looks like this:

Now, you need to find music to add to your new Playlist. To select from your entire library, click "Music" under the Library tab. To select songs from a Playlist already created, click on that playlist.

Adding Individual Songs:

Click on any individual song to select it, then keep holding down the mouse key while you drag it over to your new Playlist. To put it into the playlist, "drop it," by letting go of the mouse key when the song name you are dragging is on

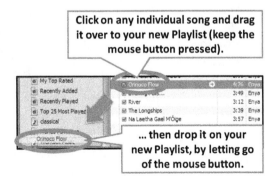

the Playlist name.

Adding Multiple Songs/Videos:

1. To add selected songs that are not all listed together, press and hold the CTRL key (Windows) or COMMAND key (Mac), then click on individual songs/videos. Once you are done selecting songs/videos, then release the CONTROL/COMMAND key.

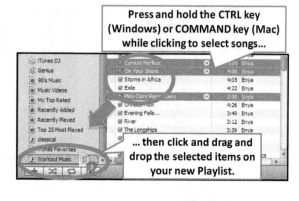

Press and hold the CTRL key (Windows) or COMMAND key (Mac) while clicking to select songs...

... then click and drag and drop the selected items on your new Playlist.

2. After all the songs/videos are selected (highlighted), click on one of the selected songs and drag and drop the entire selected group onto your Playlist.

Adding a List of Songs/Videos:

1. To add a list of songs/videos that are all together in a continuous list, press and hold the SHIFT key. Then while pressing the SHIFT key, click on the top item in the list, then click on the bottom item. All items will be selected.

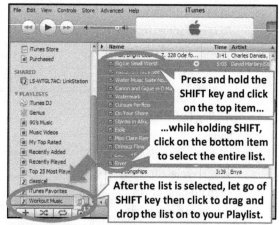

Press and hold the SHIFT key and click on the top item...

...while holding SHIFT, click on the bottom item to select the entire list.

After the list is selected, let go of SHIFT key then click to drag and drop the list on to your Playlist.

2. After all the songs/videos are selected (highlighted), click on one of the selected songs and drag and drop the entire selected group onto your Playlist.

Setting up your iPhone

Once you have iTunes set up and running on your computer and your Playlists organized, you are ready to connect your iPhone for the first time.

Plug in the white connection cable that was supplied with your iPhone to an available USB port on your computer. If iTunes is not already started, it will start automatically once you plug in the iPhone.

Can I sync using Bluetooth instead of the USB cable?

No. At the time of publishing, Bluetooth transfer speeds were too slow to allow syncing of your media to your iPhone, so Bluetooth connection for iTunes Sync is not allowed.

Windows will install the necessary drivers and then iTunes will launch the new iPhone setup screen.

Upgrading from one iPhone to a New iPhone

Step 1: If you have your old iPhone accessible, you should first do a complete backup using the steps found on page 62.
Step 2: If iTunes detects that you had another iPhone connected to your computer, it will ask you if you want to set up a new iPhone or restore from a backup of your other iPhone. Choose "restore from Backup" and follow the on-screen instructions.

From now on we will show you the screen shots of setting up a new iPhone.

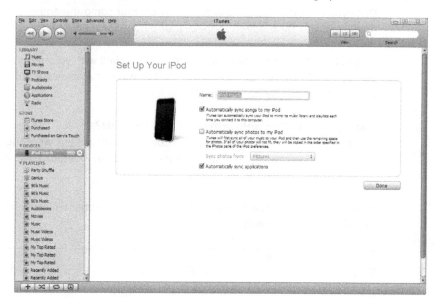

Give your iPhone a name. Each time you plug in your iPhone – to this or any other computer – your iPhone will show the name you choose here.

We will name this one "**Gary's iPhone**."

You will also see three boxes available to check – one is to automatically sync songs to your iPhone, the other is to automatically sync photos. If you are the kind of person who likes everything to be easy an automatic, and you want all of your music that is in your iTunes library on your new iPhone – then go ahead and check that box.

WARNING: Your iPhone does not have as much memory as your computer, so be careful selecting "automatically sync" when you have 1,000's of songs in your computer iTunes library.

If you like to manage your music on your own or your iPhone cannot hold your entire music library from iTunes, then don't check this "Automatically Sync Songs" box.

Follow the same rule of thumb with your pictures; if you want all your pictures on your iPhone or all pictures from a particular folder, then go ahead and check this box – otherwise, leave it blank and you can manually add pictures later on.

Lastly, if you want this computer to automatically sync applications you purchase from the App Store on your computer, then go ahead and put a check mark in the "Automatically Sync Applications" box. The advantage to this is that the applications are often updated and you can then update them in iTunes and sync the newest versions right to your iPhone.

Why do I need to buy Apps on my computer iTunes rather than just on my iPhone?

Some of the Apps are so large (800 MB or larger - example "Myst" Game) that it is not currently possible to purchase and download wirelessly, you have to load these Apps using your USB sync cable and your computer.

Once you confirm your choices, you will be taken to the main screen that you will see every time you connect your iPhone to iTunes from now on.

Create an iTunes Account or Sign In (Required to Buy Anything)

If you have music CDs that you want to load onto your iPhone, then check out our section for loading CDs on page 82. If you want to buy songs, videos and more, you will need to purchase them from the iTunes store.

In order to Sign In or create a new iTunes account, you will need to click the "Sign In" button in the upper right corner as shown below.

If you do not yet have an iTunes account, then click the "Create New Account" button and follow the instructions to create your new account. If you already have an account, then entering your Apple ID or AOL screen name and password, then click the "**Sign In**" button.

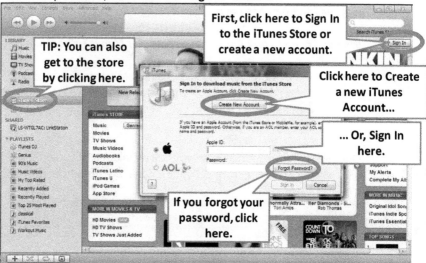

When you click on the "**Create New Account**" button, you will see a screen similar to this one:

Next, you will need to read and accept the Terms and Conditions by clicking the checkbox at the bottom of this screen:

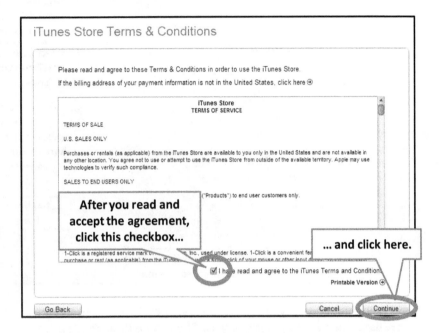

On this next screen, you setup your **Apple ID** (login name for the iTunes store), your password as well as your 'Secret Question' and email preferences. If you do not want email notification, be sure to uncheck the boxes at the bottom of the page.

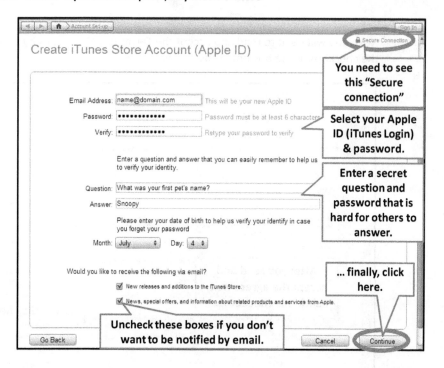

In the next screen you need to enter your preferred billing information to be used when you buy music, videos, iPhone Apps (from the App Store on your iPhone). You can also enter coupon codes, gift cards or certificates here.

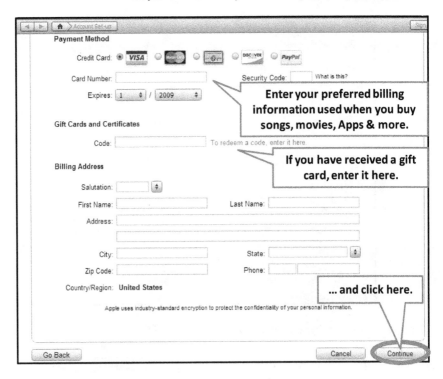

Now, depending on your locale, you may need to verify your county, province or other local taxing authority. Then click "Done."

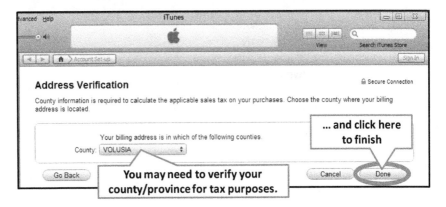

Now, you will be automatically logged in to the iTunes store with your new Apple ID. You can see when you are signed in because your Apple ID (Email address) will be shown in the upper right corner (where the "Sign In" button was located). You can always get back to the iTunes store by clicking the "iTunes Store" link under "STORE" in the left column.

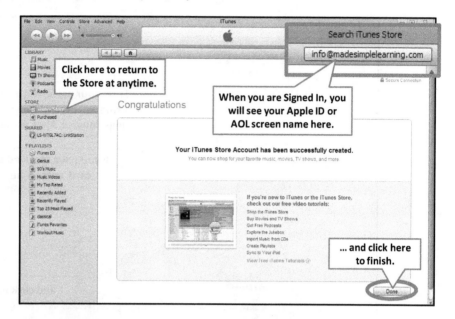

Buying Music, Videos and More from the iTunes Store

After Signing In or creating your new account, you will be able to search the store for any artist, album, composer or title.

BROWSE STORE BY GENRE:
If you prefer to browse by Genre to locate songs, just click the Genres pull down button next to "Music" in the iTunes STORE box as shown. Select the Genre you prefer.

Then the entire store will be tailored to show you songs from your selected Genre.

To find all the songs by a particular artist, type that artist name into the SEARCH box in the upper right corner. You could also search by part or all of a particular song name the same way. Once you press the ENTER key, you will be presented with all matching items from the iTunes store as shown below.

You can then navigate around and purchase individual songs with the "BUY SONG" buttons in the bottom.

After you click on "BUY SONG," you will need to login unless you specified to have iTunes keep you logged in for your purchases.

NOTE: If you are at a public computer or are worried that anyone who might access your computer (e.g. your kids, spouse, friends) would buy stuff without you knowing -- Then don't check the "Remember password for purchasing" box.

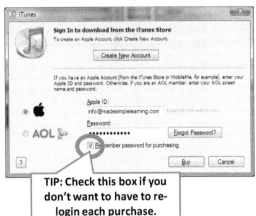

After you login, if you have just clicked "BUY," you will see this warning message.

If you don't want to see this every time, then check the box at the bottom before clicking the "BUY" button.

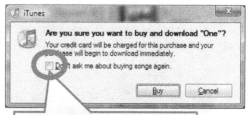

TIP: Check this box if you don't want to be asked this question for each purchase.

Now the song, video or other item you purchased will be queued up to be downloaded to your local library in iTunes on your computer. Read below to learn how to check the Download status.

Making Sure all My Purchased Items are Downloaded

After you purchase a song, video, App or other item from the Store, or if you have just Authorized this computer on your account (see page 68), you should click on the "Downloads" link that appears under the "STORE" category heading in the left column.

Any items currently being downloaded will show a status bar in the Downloads main window, and "Done" when they are completely downloaded to your computer.

You will need to see a status of "Done" before you can put the purchased item onto your iPhone.

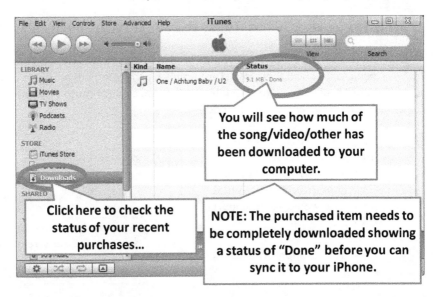

You will see how much of the song/video/other has been downloaded to your computer.

Click here to check the status of your recent purchases...

NOTE: The purchased item needs to be completely downloaded showing a status of "Done" before you can sync it to your iPhone.

If you see a pop-up asking if you want iTunes to download all your Purchased items, click "YES."

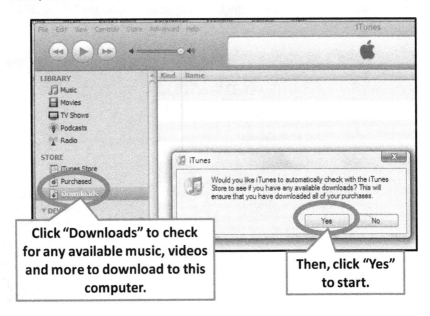

Click "Downloads" to check for any available music, videos and more to download to this computer.

Then, click "Yes" to start.

Loading My Music CDs into iTunes so I can put them on my iPhone

If you have Music CDs that you want to load up onto your iPhone, you will need to first load them into iTunes, then use the methods we describe in this book to move them to your iPhone. (See page 72 for "Auto Sync" or page 86 for the "Drag and Drop" method.)

First, start up iTunes. Then, insert the CD into your computer's CD drive. You may see a pop-up inside iTunes that asks if you would like to import the CD as shown.

Click "Yes" to import the CD.

After you insert the CD, you may see this screen pop-up, click "Yes" to Import into iTunes.

If you did not receive this pop-up window, then you can manually start the CD import into iTunes by clicking the Import CD button in the lower right corner. You will also notice that the CD has appeared under the "DEVICES" list in the left column.

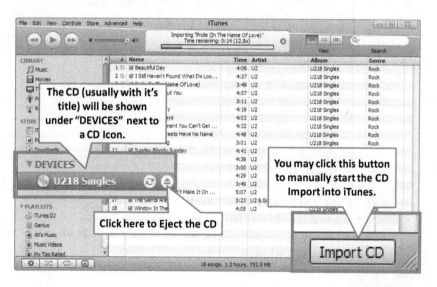

The CD (usually with it's title) will be shown under "DEVICES" next to a CD Icon.

Click here to Eject the CD

You may click this button to manually start the CD Import into iTunes.

Import CD

Redeeming an iTunes Gift Card

You may sometime receive an iTunes Gift Card, here we show you how to add it to your iTunes account so you can buy music, videos and more with its value.

First, click the "iTunes Store" link in the left column, then click the "Redeem" in the "QUICK LINKS" box on the right side.

On the next "Redeem" screen, you will need to enter the code from the back of the Gift Card. (You may need to scratch off the silver/gray covering to see the code.) Then click the "Redeem" button.

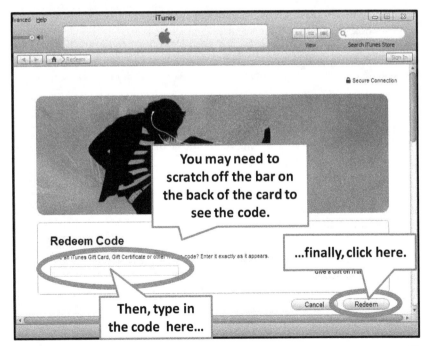

Then, in order to verify that the Gift Card is being applied to the correct iTunes account, you will need to Sign In or re-enter your password.

Click "Sign In" or "View Account" (if already Signed In).

Finally, when the Gift Card has been successfully applied to your account you will see the total amount of the card in the upper right corner of the iTunes screen next to your sign-in name. Now you can use this Gift Card credit to buy stuff from iTunes.

Manually Putting Music, Movies, Podcasts and More on My iPhone ("Drag & Drop" Method)

If you checked the "Automatically Sync Music" box, then you will see the message window in iTunes showing you that your music was Synchronizing.

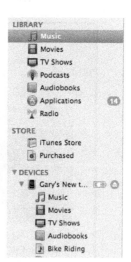

If you chose to "manually" sync your music (by leaving the checkbox unchecked) -- you will then have to drag and drop songs, videos or Playlists onto your iPhone to get music or videos onto the iPhone.

Many of us who use iTunes to manage our music already have music loaded into iTunes before we get an iPhone.

When your iPhone is connected, you will see it listed in the left hand column under "Devices."

Use the same techniques as we showed above when you added songs to a new Playlist to add songs to your iPhone.

SELECTING AND MOVING SONGS (NOT IN A LIST):
have found music that I want to put onto my iPhone. I select the songs (or albums) I want to move onto my iPhone by holding down the "Ctrl" button (Windows) or "Command" button (Mac) while I use my mouse and left-click (Single click for Mac) on each song. The highlighted songs will turn blue.

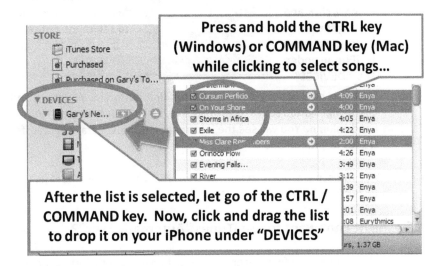

SELECTING AND MOVING SONGS/VIDEOS IN A LIST:
To highlight an entire album or many songs listed in a row – for example all songs by a particular artist – hold down the "Shift" key (Windows and Mac) and click (left-click in Windows) the top of the list – then go all the way to the bottom of the list you want to copy – go to the last song (keeping the shift key down) and left click again. All the songs between those two points will turn blue.

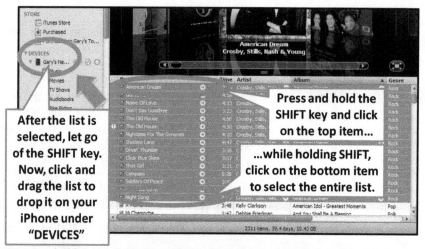

After the list is selected, let go of the SHIFT key. Now, click and drag the list to drop it on your iPhone under "DEVICES"

Press and hold the SHIFT key and click on the top item...

...while holding SHIFT, click on the bottom item to select the entire list.

Now, just hold down the Mouse button (left button for Windows) and "Drag" all the highlighted songs to your iPhone, listed under "Devices" in the left hand column. You will see the information window detail the transfer from iTunes to your iPhone.

Use this same process to transfer Movies, TV shows and Podcasts and Audio Books from your iTunes directory right onto your iPhone.

Why might I not want to use iTunes "Automatic Sync"?

There could be a few reasons to manually sync, but the primary one is this: If you put all your Music, Videos, etc. onto your iPhone you will run out of room for important stuff like: your email and all those fun Apps from the App Store!

Automatically Synchronizing your Music and Videos to your iPhone

If you selected the "Automatically Synchronize" as shown on page 73, you will see a "Synchronizing iPhone" message window at the top if iTunes showing you the status of the sync process.

How can I stop the Sync process to my iPhone?

Sometimes you might want to cancel the sync process to your iPhone. In order to do this you will need to click on the small "x" in the "Command Box" which shows the Syncing information.

You can also Hold down the Command + Option (Mac) or Shift + Ctrl (Windows) keys while connecting your iPod. This will turn off Auto Sync.

Can I 'Authorize' more than one computer to play my iTunes media?

Yes, you can "Authorize" up to 5 different computers to play your iTunes media (music, movies, etc.).

Someone else has Authorized my computer to play their songs, can I now load and listen to these 'authorized songs' onto my iPhone?
The short answer is "Maybe."
The answer is "NO" for all songs purchased on iTunes earlier than January 2009 and all songs purchased with "DRM" (Digital Rights Management) protection. These songs are tied specifically to one person's iPod/iPhone.
The answer is "YES" for all songs purchased without DRM Protection enabled. Early in 2009, iTunes announced that it would start selling some songs and videos without DRM Protection, which means they could be played on multiple iPods and iPhones.
As we, Made Simple Learning, are creators of intellectual property - books and videos, we don't advocate sharing purchased music, please pay the artist, author or video producer what they deserve - so they can keep making great songs, books and videos!

Start up iTunes and go to the "**Store**" menu and select "**Authorize Computer...**"

NOTE: You will need to know your iTunes or AOL Username and Password for this to work.

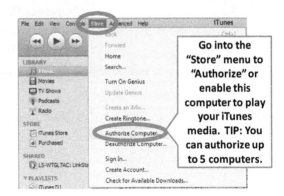

Go into the "Store" menu to "Authorize" or enable this computer to play your iTunes media. TIP: You can authorize up to 5 computers.

Enter your Apple ID or, if you prefer, click the radio button next to AOL and enter your AOL screen name and password.

Then click the "Authorize" button.

How do I "Get Album Artwork" in iTunes?

iTunes may automatically get the Album Art for most songs and videos, however, if you need to manually retrieve this Artwork, then follow these steps. *NOTE: You will need to already have an iTunes account and login for this to work correctly.*

Start up iTunes and go to the "**Advanced**" menu and select "**Get Album Artwork**"

How to Turn Off or Disable the "Automatic Sync"

If you had selected "Automatically Synchronize" media and want to turn this feature off see Page 72

Finding Songs and Videos Using the Search Box in iTunes

If your library is not already hundreds or thousands of songs and other media, it will be soon! How do you quickly find that special song you are in the mood for right now? The quickest way to locate an individual song or video is to use the "Search" bar in the upper right corner of iTunes.

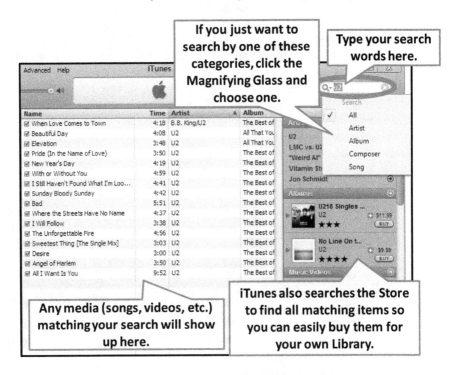

If you just want to search by one of these categories, click the Magnifying Glass and choose one.

Type your search words here.

Any media (songs, videos, etc.) matching your search will show up here.

iTunes also searches the Store to find all matching items so you can easily buy them for your own Library.

In the Search window Just start typing any part of the following categories to find the item:

- Artist Name
- Album Name
- Composer
- Song/Video Name

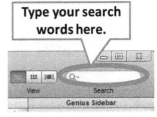

Type your search words here.

You will notice that as soon as you type the first letter, iTunes will narrow your search results (shown in the main window) by that letter. What it is doing is finding all matching songs/videos that have the letter (or series of letters) matching any part of the Artist, Album, Composer or Song/Video name.

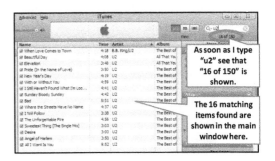

As soon as I type "u2" see that "16 of 150" is shown.

The 16 matching items found are shown in the main window here.

SEARCH TIP
You can type any combination of words to match the item you are trying to find. For example, if you know that the song has the word "Love" in the title and the song is by the Artist "U2" - you would just type in the two words separated by a SPACE: "Love U2" and immediately be shown all matching items. In this case, only 2 songs matched, so I can quickly double click on the song I wanted to listen to.

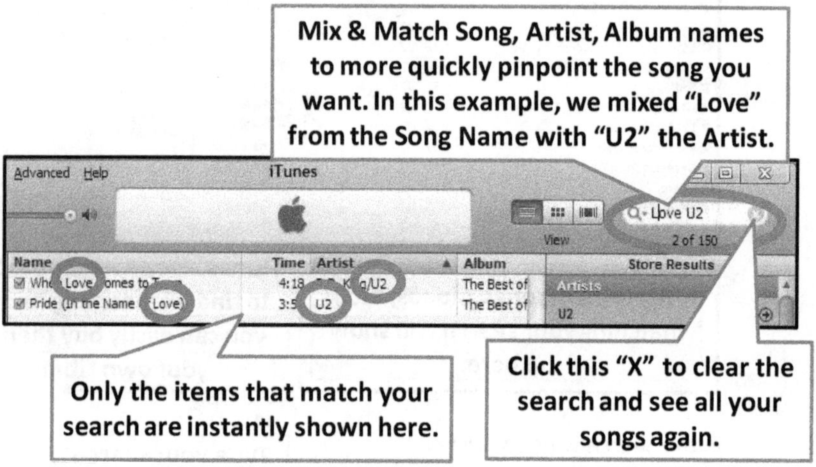

Mix & Match Song, Artist, Album names to more quickly pinpoint the song you want. In this example, we mixed "Love" from the Song Name with "U2" the Artist.

Only the items that match your search are instantly shown here.

Click this "X" to clear the search and see all your songs again.

When you are done searching, just hit the little "X" in the circle next to the search words to clear out the search and see all your songs and videos again.

Changing Views in iTunes (List, Grid or Cover Flow)

There are many ways to view your music, videos and other media in iTunes on your computer. Getting familiar with these views on your computer will help you because you will notice that your iPhone also has many of the same views. There are three primary views, which can be further customized, called "List View," "Grid View," and "Cover Flow."

LIST VIEW:
Click the left-most icon of the three view icons to see List View. You can re-sort the list by any column by clicking on that column heading. For example, to sort by "Name" you would click on the "Name" column heading. To reverse the sort order, just click the same column heading again.

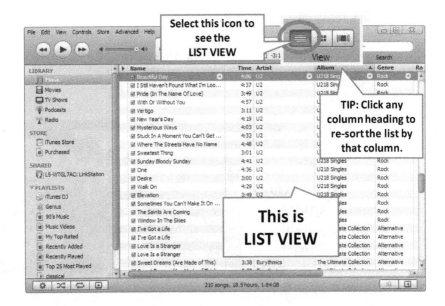

GRID VIEW:

COVER FLOW VIEW:

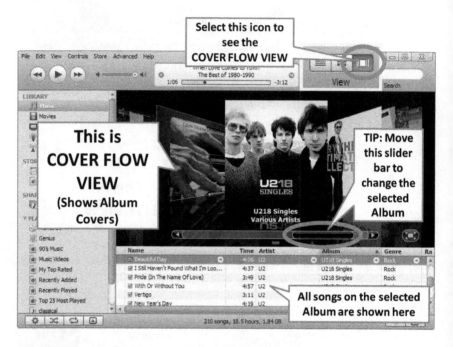

Transferring or Syncing Contacts, Calendar and Notes

Think of your iPhone like a mini-computer in your hand. It is just about as powerful and capable as a laptop computer. One of the things that the iPhone does well is help you manage your work and personal life by holding all your contacts, most up-to-date calendar and notes. What's even better is that all that information is synchronized (or shared) with your PC or Mac using iTunes.

I want to use wireless synchronization or sharing of my contacts and calendar - with my iPhone what are my options?
NOTE: You can setup wireless access to your Contacts and Calendars if you have one of the following environments:

Your Environment	Wireless Sync Using	Notes
Google Calendar and Contacts in Gmail	Google Sync for iPhone m.google.com/sync	This is free.
LDAP (Lightweight Directory Access Protocol) Contacts	Built-in Sync software in Settings > Mail,Contacts,Calendar>Add Account > Other > Add LDAP Account	This is free.
CalDAV Calendar Account	Built-in Sync software in Settings > Mail,Contacts,Calendar>Add Account > Other > Add CalDAV Account	This is Free. Must have access to CalDAV account in this format cal.server.com with a Username & Password
Subscribed Calendar at your work	Built-in Sync software in Settings > Mail,Contacts,Calendar>Add Account > Other > Add Subscribed Calendar	This is Free. Must have access to a subscribed calendar (Web address, username & Password) Access to server is in this format: myserver.com/cal.ics
Calendars and Contacts Stored at www.me.com (What Apple calls "cloud" synchronization)	Mobile Me Using Web Based Address Book and Calendar, information is "pushed" to your iPhone automatically and changes made on iPhone are automatically reflected in web based programs.	Free 60 days, then $99 / year after that.

To setup this synchronization you need to get into the "Info" tab of your iPhone inside iTunes. To get there, first click on your iPhone listed under the DEVICES section in the left column, then click on the "Info" tab along the top.

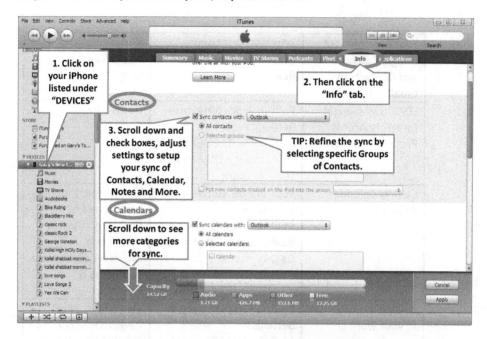

As you scroll down, you will see that sections to setup the sync for your "Contacts," "Calendars," "Mail Accounts," "Web Browser" and an "Advanced" section.

Each section has a little checkbox that you can check in order to sync the selected information with your iPhone. Under "Contacts" you can choose with which PC program to sync the contacts on your iPhone. If you are a Microsoft Outlook user, choose "Outlook." If you use Windows Contacts or any other program, choose it from the drop down list.

SYNC ONLY SPECIFIC GROUPS
If you only want selected groups on your iPhone, choose the radio button for "Selected Groups" and then choose the specific groups you wish to Sync to you iPhone.

WHAT YOU SEE WILL VARY BY WHAT IS INSTALLED ON YOUR COMPUTER:
The options you see presented inside iTunes will vary depending on what software is installed on your computer. For example, if you have installed Google Sync software, you will see a new option allowing you to "Sync Google Contacts" as shown:

If you are a Mac user, the various Mac programs for calendar management will be listed that are installed on your computer. For example, if you use a program like Pocket Mac it will be listed as an option.

Follow the same procedure for your Calendar. If you have multiple calendars on your PC – you can choose exactly which ones you with to Sync.

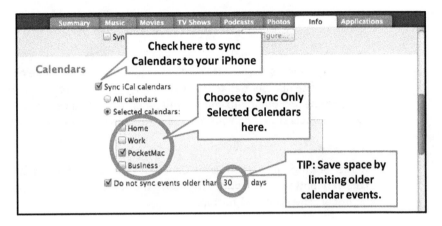

NOTE: For Mac users – If you use Microsoft Entourage, you will need to enable Entourage to Sync with iCal. You do this by going into the Preferences Settings in Entourage and then going to "Sync Services" checking off the radio box that says synchronize with "iCal" and Address book.

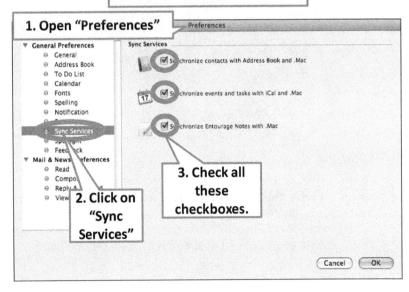

MULTIPLE CALENDARS NOT SUPPORTED IN ENTOURAGE:
Be aware that as of the writing of this book, Entourage, unlike iCal, cannot handle multiple calendars –so, if you have various separate calendars, they will not show up in Entourage.

Importing SIM Card Contacts

Sometimes, on another mobile phone, you may have saved contact names and phone numbers to your SIM card. (The SIM card is the unique card that has your phone number tied to it.) If you took your SIM card out of your old mobile phone and put it into your iPhone, then you would be able to import all your contacts stored on your old SIM card into your iPhone contact list icon.

Tap the "Settings" icon, then "Mail, Contacts, Calendars." Scroll down almost to the very bottom of the page (just above the "Calendars" section) and tap the "Import SIM Contacts" button.

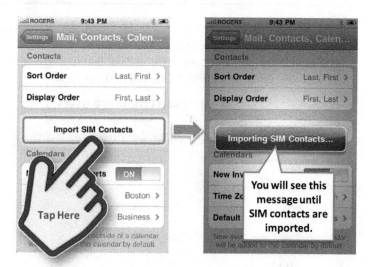

WARNING: Unless you have specifically arranged with your phone company to insert your old SIM card into your iPhone and use it with your iPhone, you should probably remove it and replace it with the SIM card that came with your iPhone. The reason is this: your old SIM card may not be correctly setup or "provisioned" in cell phone terms to handle your iPhone data plan. This could result in you being surprised by a really high cell phone bill.

To Replace all Contacts and Calendar Entries on Your iPhone

If you ever need to "Start Over" on your iPhone or just want to replace your contacts and calendar items with those from your computer, just scroll down to the "Advanced" section in the "Info" tab. Check those items you desire to be replaced (overwritten) on your iPhone. This is useful if your computer information is up to date and you just want to transfer it all to your new iPhone (and erase what was originally on the iPhone).

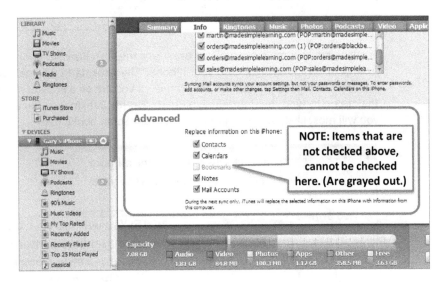

Setting Up Email Accounts on Your iPhone

You can use iTunes to setup your Email accounts for full wireless access on your iPhone by scrolling down to the "Mail Accounts" section of the "Info" sync section.

BENEFIT TO YOU: if you Sync your email accounts through iTunes, you will not need to set up your email account manually on the iPhone itself. Just select which email accounts you want to be automatically set up on your iPhone.

NOTE: All account settings will be synced and installed on your iPhone, but not your passwords for each account; you will need to enter those manually only once, the first time, you check mail on your iPhone.

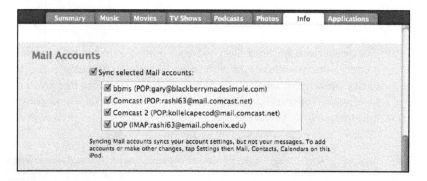

Scrolling down some more you can even sync the Web Browser bookmarks from your computer right onto your iPhone. The bookmarks will then be set right into the Safari browser on the iPhone. If you are on a PC, you might see the option to sync your Internet Explorer or Firefox Bookmarks. On a Mac, you will most likely see the option to sync your Safari bookmarks.

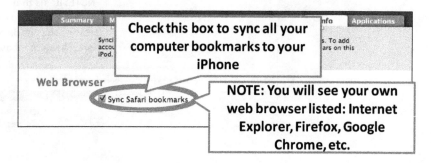

Sync Movies Automatically

When you click the "Movies" tab, you can choose to Sync specific movies or all of them.

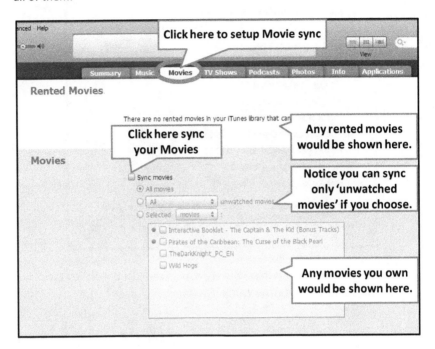

Transferring Photos

If I click on the "Photos" tab, I will see a radio box I can check to sync my photos from a particular folder. In Windows, the default is usually "My Pictures" but I can use the drop down menu to select the correct program in which to find my photo library.

I can then choose to sync all my photos (which would be way too many for my iPhone) or just selected folders. Each folder and the number of pictures inside are listed for me to check.

TIP: Learn how to manually transfer photos from your iPhone to your computer (PC or Mac) on page 134.

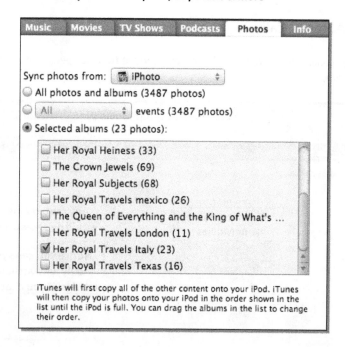

Once I select the photos I wish to Sync, I can just press the "Sync" button and they will be transferred to my iPhone.

Manually Transferring "Dragging & Dropping" Movies, TV Shows, Podcasts, Audio Books and more to your iPhone

The process to manually add or remove Movies, TV Shows, Podcasts is the same as we show on page 86 to manually transfer songs to your iPhone.

Example:
To transfer a specific movie you would:

Click on the "Movies" tab in the left column under "LIBRARY" to see your movies.

Click and drag a single movie or several selected movies (learn how to select multiple movies in a row or separately on page 84) and drop it on your iPhone under DEVICES.

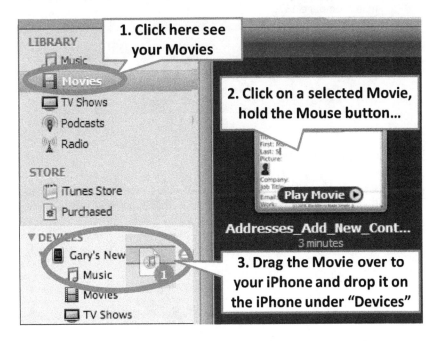

Once the movie (or movies) have been 'dropped' on your iPhone then just press the "Sync" button at the bottom right and the selected media will be synced right to my iPhone.

Chapter 4:
Using Your iPhone as a Phone

The iPhone is capable of so many things that it is often easy to forget the fact that it is also a phone. The iPhone is packed with features you would expect from a high end Smartphone.

Getting Started with Phone Features

The iPhone initially places the Phone icon at the furthest left point of the bottom dock. You can move this icon somewhere else, just look at "Moving Icons" on page 157.

To place a Call From the Keypad

Just touch the "Phone" icon and you will be taken into your Phone App. The first thing you will notice is the bottom row of icons or soft keys – very much like those in other iPhone applications.

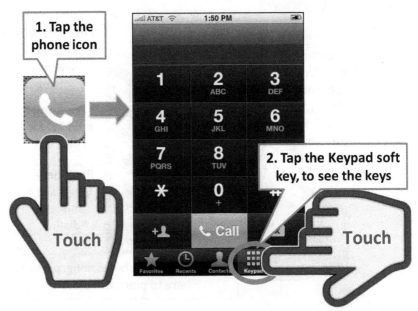

1. Tap the phone icon

Touch

2. Tap the Keypad soft key, to see the keys

Touch

There are icons along the bottom for "Favorites," "Recents," "Contacts," "Keypad" and "Voicemail."

Once you press the Keypad softkey, then you can dial the phone normally. If you make a mistake, press the backspace key in the lower right corner.

TIP: If you need to dial a phone number with an extension, then press and hold the asterisk key (*) to see a comma (,) - this is a 2 second pause, then dial the extension. This will save you time from waiting to dial someone's extension.

TIP: If you need to dial a plus sign (+) for international country codes, then press and hold the zero key (0) to type the plus.

Press and hold * for a 2 second pause (,) -- useful for dialing extensions.

If the person is in your Address Book, you will see their name appear.

Press and hold "0" for a plus sign

Press here if you make a mistake dialing

Touch

Once you are finished dialing, press here to place the call.

When you are done dialing, just tap the Call button to start the call.

Placing Calls from Contacts

One of the great things about having all your contact information in your phone is that it is very easy to place calls from your "Contacts" on the iPhone.

The easiest way to do this is to start the "Phone" App and then touch the "Contacts" icon along the bottom row.

Just scroll through your contacts or search your contacts as you did on Page 248.

When you find the contact you are searching for, just touch the entry and their contact information will be displayed on the screen.

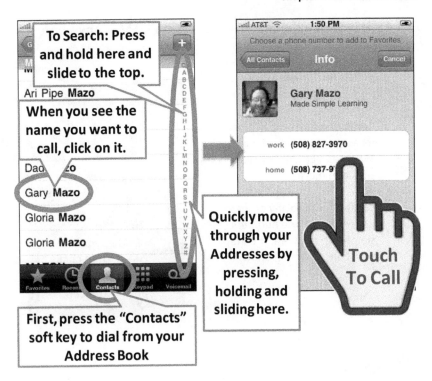

To Search: Press and hold here and slide to the top.

When you see the name you want to call, click on it.

Ari Pipe **Mazo**

Dad **Mazo**

Gary **Mazo**

Gloria **Mazo**

Gloria **Mazo**

Quickly move through your Addresses by pressing, holding and sliding here.

First, press the "Contacts" soft key to dial from your Address Book

Favorites   Recent   Contacts   Keypad   Voicemail

Choose a phone number to add to Favorites

All Contacts   Info   Cancel

Gary Mazo
Made Simple Learning

work   (508) 827-3970

home   (508) 737-9

Touch To Call

Just touch the number you wish to dial – if a contact has several numbers, just touch the one you want to call. As soon as you touch the number, the phone call will be initiated.

Call Any Underlined Phone Number (Email, SMS, Anywhere)

You will notice that the iPhone underlines almost every phone number it 'sees' on the screen.

Common places are in email messages (people's signatures), SMS messages, notes, web sites and more.

To start a call to any of these underlined phone numbers, simply tap on them, then tap the "Call" button as shown.

Voice Dialing

While the iPhone does not come with built-in voice dialing, you can get some great Apps from the App Store to provide you with robust voice dialing.

We tested one free App called "VoiceBox Dialer(TM)" and found that it worked quite well. You can dial by name, number, access **"Recents"** and **"Favorites"** right from the application.

FAQ: Does the iPhone 3G have a Voice Dialing Feature?
No. As of publishing time, the iPhone 3G does not support voice dialing, however the new iPhone 3G S – not covered in this book – does.

Setting "Favorites" aka "Speed Dial" on your iPhone

The icon furthest to the left of the bottom row of icons is entitled "Favorites." This is a place where you can store numbers you call most often for easy retrieval and calling.

It is much easier to save frequently called numbers to **"Favorites"** than have to search through your contacts each time you want to call the frequently called contact.

Adding Your "Favorites"

Touch the **"Favorites"** icon. When you first start up **"Favorites"** it will show a blank screen. Just touch the small Blue "+" sign in the upper right hand corner. Your contact directory will open.

As you did before, search for the contact that you wish to place in your "Favorites" directory.

If the contact has more than one number associated with it, the contact screen will open and you can just touch the number you wish to be listed under the **"Favorites"** category.

If there is only one number associated with the contact, you will see it load right into the **"Favorites."** Next to the entry it will also tell you which number – mobile, work or home you have set as the favorite number.

Calling a "Favorite"

To call a **"Favorite,"** just touch the name of the individual. There is no prompt or confirmation, as soon as you touch his or her name, the phone will dial.

Editing Your Favorites

If at any time you want to change or edit a **"Favorite"** entry, just touch **"Edit"** in the top left hand corner.   Just like other applications with an **"Edit"** feature, there will now be a red "-"sign next to each entry.

Touch the "-"sign and you will see a **"Delete"** button appear. Just tap that button to remove the entry from Favorites.

Then click the "Done" button in the upper right corner when you are finished.

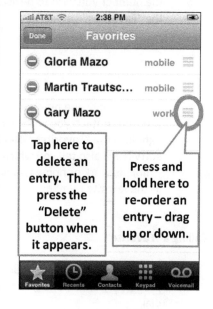

TIP: To re-order your favorites, just press and hold the three bars on the right side of each entry. _work_ ☰ Then drag the name up or down the list.

Using Recents (Think "Call Logs")

Using **"Recents"** is like looking at your "Call Log" on other smartphones.

When you touch the **"Recents"** icon, a list of all your recent calls will be listed. You can touch the **"All"** or **"Missed"** button at the top to narrow down the list.

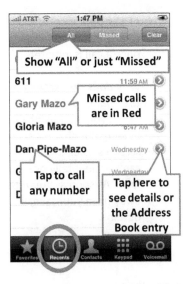

Show "All" or just "Missed"

Missed calls are in Red

Tap to call any number

Tap here to see details or the Address Book entry

To Place a Call from Recents

Just touch the name or phone number and the iPhone will immediately begin to initiate a phone call to the individual.

Clear Out all Recents

To clear or erase all your recent call log entries, press the "Clear" button in the upper right corner.

To Look at Details of a Call or Contact Information

Touch the Blue Arrow next to the name and you will see the full "Contact Information" for that particular contact if they are in your Address Book. Otherwise, you will see details of this entry.

11:44 AM

Options While on a Call

All the phone options available to you are clearly indicated in the "Options" screen once a call is initiated.

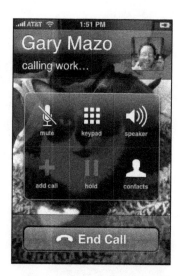

Why does the screen go blank when I hold the phone to my ear?
When you are talking into the iPhone holding the phone next to your face, the screen senses this and goes blank so you can't accidentally press a button with your face. As soon as you move the iPhone away from your face, you will see the options.

Muting the Call

As the number is dialing, you will see the option in the top left row to "Mute" the call. Just press the **"Mute"** button to mute yourself.

Using the Keypad

Perhaps the number you call requires you to then input an extension. Or, perhaps you are calling an automated answering service that requires you to input numbers for choices.

In these situations, just touch the **"Keypad"** icon and the keypad will be displayed. Just input numbers as prompted.

Then press the **"Hide Keypad"** button at the bottom when done.

Using the Speaker Phone

If you would prefer to use the built in Speaker Phone on the iPhone, just touch the **"Speaker"** icon.

Tap that same icon again to turn off the Speakerphone.

Putting the Call on "Hold"

Perhaps you need to put your call on "Hold" to look up contact information for someone else or to initiate a "conference" call – see page 115.

Just touch the **"Hold"** button and the current call will be put on **"Hold"** until you tap the same button again to continue the call.

Looking through Contacts

Let's say you need to browse through your **"Contacts"** while on a call – after all, we are a multi-tasking society! Just touch the **"Contacts"** button and scroll through or search for a contact.

NOTE: it is a good idea to use the Speakerphone or a Bluetooth Headset while doing this (see page 140) so you can continue to talk on the phone while searching for the contact.

Setting up and Using Voicemail or Visual Voicemail

You have two options for Voicemail on the iPhone; the first is the standard, included Voicemail option and the second is the iPhone "Enhanced" voicemail service.

"Enhanced" Voicemail is often called "Visual Voicemail" and is a great option for about $1.99 a month extra.

Setting up "Standard" voicemail

When you touch your "Voicemail" icon for the first time, you will be asked to call your voice mailbox and choose a password and record a greeting. Just follow the voice prompts.

Once your Voicemail is set up, just touch the Voicemail icon to call and retrieve Voicemail in the future.

Using "Enhanced" Voicemail

This is a subscription service that needs to be active in order to set up. You will be prompted on the screen to pick a password and then re-enter the password.

Next, you can choose a "Standard" greeting or "Record" a new one.

The "Standard" greeting will say your phone number in a computer voice and that you are not available.

If you choose **"Record,"** you just speak into the phone and record your personal voicemail greeting. The screen indicates that you are recording your Voicemail. Just press red **"Stop"** Button when you are done.

Listening to your Greeting

Once recorded, you have the option to **"Play"** and listen to your greeting or to **"Record"** a new greeting.

Playing your Voicemail

The beauty of the "Enhanced" voicemail is that you never have to call in to check your voicemail. All Voicemail messages will reside on your phone. You can save them, scroll through them or delete them.

The voicemail icon will show the number of Voicemails you have in your mailbox. Just touch the **"Play"** button and the message will play through your handset.

To Hear Message through the Speaker

If you would like to hear your voicemail through the iPhone's speaker (as opposed to listening through the handset) just touch the "Speaker" button in the upper right hand corner.

To Adjust the "Greeting"

If you would like to change your greeting, just touch the **"Greeting"** button. You can listen to your greeting again or record a new one or change the greeting back to the "Default" if you would prefer.

To "Call Back" the Person that left you the Voice Mail

Just touch the **"Call Back"** button and you can immediately return the call of the individual who left you the voicemail.

To "Delete" the Voicemail

Your iPhone will store all your voicemails if you like to save them and listen at a later date. Sometimes, Voicemails can get a bit unwieldy if you have too many of them. Just touch the red **"Delete"** button and the message will be "Deleted."

NOTE: you still have the option to "Save" a "Deleted" message. Your Voicemail screen will show your "Deleted" messaged in its own tab. Touch a "Deleted" message and you can then "Undelete" to restore it.

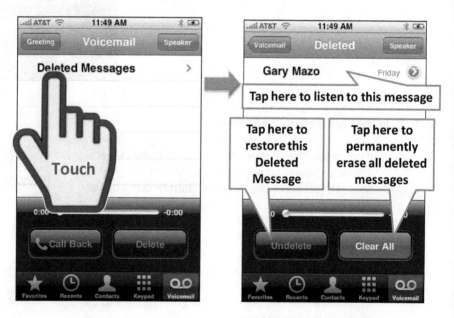

If you would like to permanently "Delete" the message, just touch **"Clear All."**

Chapter 5:
Advanced Phone Topics

Now that you have the basic phone feature down, it is time to explore the more advanced capabilities of the phone on the iPhone. In this chapter we will look at working with multiple callers and setting up Conference calling. We will also show you how to "Forward" your phone calls to another number. Lastly, we will show you how set separate "Ring Tones" for individual callers.

Conference Calling

In today's busy world, working with several callers at once has become something that we demand from our Phones. Fortunately, Conference calling is very intuitive on the iPhone.

Initiating the First Call

As we showed you in the previous chapter, just make a call to any number – a contact, a new number – anyone at all.

Move the call away from your face and you will see the phone "Menu" of options available to you. Most of these we covered in the last chapter.

Adding a Second Caller

Touch the **"+"** sign to add a second caller. This will immediately put the first caller on "hold."

Touching the **"Add Caller"** button will bring you to your "Contacts." Just scroll or search for the contact to add to this call.

You can also add a new caller by choosing from your **"Favorites," "Recents,"** or even dialing their phone number **"Keypad"** by pressing that soft key on the bottom.

If the contact has more than one phone entry, you can just touch on the one you would like to call and the call will be initiated.

Merging Calls

Once the call to the second caller has been initiated, just move the phone away from your face and you will notice that the **"Add Caller"** button has now been replace with a **"Merge Calls"** button. Just touch the **"Merge Calls"** button and both calls will be merged into a three-way "Conference Call."

Join callers in the conference call

Speak with the other caller who is on "HOLD"

Tap here to talk privately with one caller.

Add more callers to the conference

The top of the screen will now show that you are in a "Conference" call.

Separating the Calls / To talk Privately with someone in a Conference call

In order to speak to one caller individually or privately from a conference call, touch the small arrow next to word "Conference" at the top

When you touch the arrow, you will be brought to a screen showing each caller with whom you are connected.

You can make either one of the calls "Private" by just touching the **"Private"** button. The other call will be put on hold.

You can also "Hang Up" on either call by just touching the red "Disconnect" button.

Call Forwarding

There may be times when you need to "Forward" your calls to another number. Perhaps you are traveling to a friend's house and you want to forward calls to their "land line" because they don't have good cell reception.

Just touch the "**Settings**" icon and enter the "**Phone**" settings menu. The first option under "Calls" is "Call Forwarding. Touch the "**Call Forwarding**" tab.

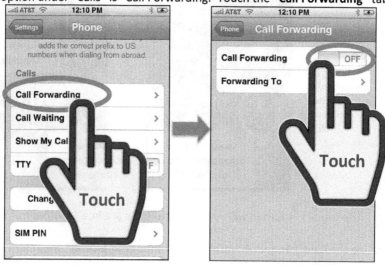

Tap the switch to change it to **"ON"** to enable Call forwarding. Once you set the switch to **"ON,"** you will be taken to the next screen. Just input the "Forwarding" number using the keypad.

Once input, the number will be stored for future reference and all calls will be forwarded from your regular iPhone number to that number until you turn call forwarding **"OFF."**

BE AWARE: Call forwarding is not always free. Check with your cell provider and see what, if any charges you will incur by enabling "Call Forwarding."

Call Waiting

Call waiting simply alerts you to the fact that another call is coming in while you are on the phone.

You then have the option to take the new call, hang up on the first call or use "Hold" and set up a "Conference Call" as you did above.

You just need to make sure the **"Call Waiting"** switch is set to the **"ON"** position, which is the default setting.

Show or Block (Hide) Your Caller ID

You have the option with the iPhone to "Block" your caller ID phone number if you choose. There may be certain situations where you would prefer that your phone number not show up on the caller's phone. Just move this switch from the default **"ON"** position to **"OFF"** to turn this feature off.

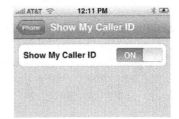

Setting Security on your SIM card - Assigning a PIN Code

As an added measure of security, you can enable a PIN code to access information stored on your SIM card. If your iPhone were ever lost or stolen, this would prevent anyone from accessing names and numbers stored on your SIM card.

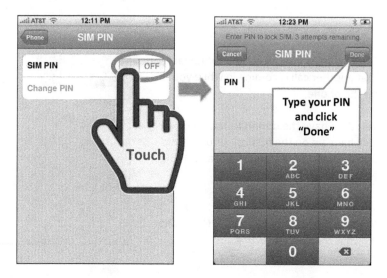

Just move the switch to the **"ON"** position and type in a four-digit PIN code. Finally click **"Done."**

AT&T (or other Carrier) Services

In the United States, as of publishing of this book, AT&T is the sole wirelessly carrier for the iPhone.

If you are not in the US, then you will have another carrier who provides your iPhone service. The button will say your wireless carrier/phone company name instead of AT&T.

Touching this tab gives you access to special numbers to check your balance, minutes used or other features.

Ring Tones, Sounds and Vibration

The iPhone can alert you to incoming calls, voice mails received and other features with unique sounds or vibrations. These can easily be adjusted using the "Settings" Icon.

Changing the Default Ring Tone

There is one "Ring Tone" that the iPhone uses as the "Default" tone. This tone will be played for all calls that come in unless you give a contact a unique "Ring Tone" which we will discuss further on in this chapter.

Go to your **"Settings"** Icon and touch the **"Sounds"** tab. You will notice the **"Ring Tone"** tab about mid-way down the screen. The "Default" tone is listed. Just touch the tab and scroll through all the available "Ring Tones."

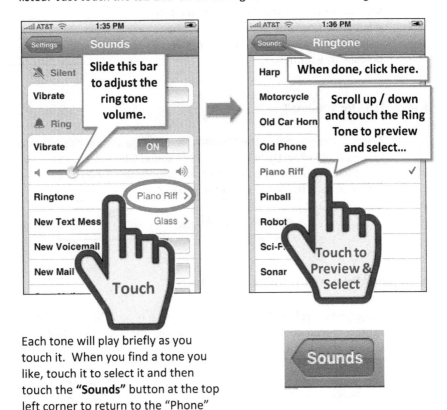

Each tone will play briefly as you touch it. When you find a tone you like, touch it to select it and then touch the **"Sounds"** button at the top left corner to return to the "Phone" settings menu.

To adjust the volume of the phone ring tone, just slide the bar below the Vibrate switch.

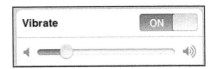

Adding "Vibration" to the Ring

The first two switches in the **"Sounds"** menu deal with "Vibration." Sometimes, your phone might be in your pocket and having a vibration in addition to a tone might be helpful to make sure you know the phone is ringing when you are in loud surroundings.

The first switch allows "Vibration" to be used in **"Silent"** mode – see page 32. The second switch tells the iPhone to vibrate in addition to ring when a call comes in. Just move either switch to the **"ON"** or **"OFF"** position as your desire.

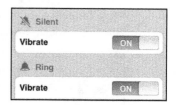

Audible Tone for Voicemail

Towards the bottom of the **"Sounds"** menu page are a series of switches. The first is to allow the iPhone to play a sound when you have a new Voicemail. You cannot adjust the tone played, only whether you would like a sound or not. The default position is **"ON."**

Assigning Unique Ringtones to Contacts

Sometimes, it is both fun and useful to give a unique "Ring Tone" to a certain contact in your address book. This way, you know who is calling without looking at your phone.

For example, one of the authors (Gary) sets the ring tone for his son Daniel to the ring tone of Elton John's "Daniel." It is easy to know immediately when he is calling. Later in this chapter we will show you how to make a ring tone from your iTunes music.

Giving a Contact a Unique Ringtone

Open the "Contact" – and look for the contact you want to change (in this case Daniel). Next to the "Ringtone" tab it says, "Default." I want to change that to a unique ring tone, so I touch the tab to see all the available tones.

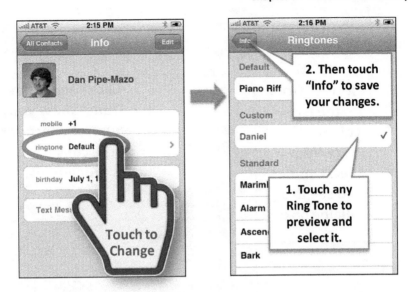

In this case, we have one "Custom" tone (you will not see this "Custom" category unless you have created your own custom ring tones.) We want the tone called "Daniel" so we tap on it to listen to it and select it. In the next section, we will show how to make custom ringtones – but you can choose any of your ringtones and assign them to a particular contact.

Creating Ringtones from your Music

Your iTunes library is filled with all your favorite songs. Wouldn't it be great if you could turn your own songs into ringtones for your iPhone? The good news is that you can turn most of your music into a ringtone. There is an "easy" way to do this (that will cost about $1 / ring tone) and a "more challenging" way to do this (which is free) – we will show you both.

"Easy Way" to Create Ringtones - Use iTunes

Before we can create Ringtones from the iTunes Store, we need to adjust a few settings in iTunes itself. From your iTunes menu, select **"View"** along the top menu and then choose **"View Options."**

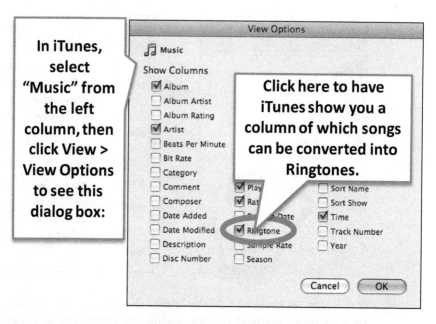

In iTunes, select "Music" from the left column, then click View > View Options to see this dialog box:

View Options

Music

Show Columns

Click here to have iTunes show you a column of which songs can be converted into Ringtones.

- ☑ Album
- ☐ Album Artist
- ☐ Album Rating
- ☑ Artist
- ☐ Beats Per Minute
- ☐ Bit Rate
- ☐ Category
- ☐ Comment
- ☐ Composer
- ☐ Date Added
- ☐ Date Modified
- ☐ Description
- ☐ Disc Number

- ☑ Play
- ☑ Rat
- ☐ Date
- ☑ Ringtone
- Sample Rate
- ☐ Season

- ☐ Sort Name
- ☐ Sort Show
- ☑ Time
- ☐ Track Number
- ☐ Year

Cancel   OK

Check off the box that next to "Ringtone" to show you a column for those songs that can be "converted" to Ringtones in iTunes.

After making this selection, you may see the following dialogue box open in iTunes:

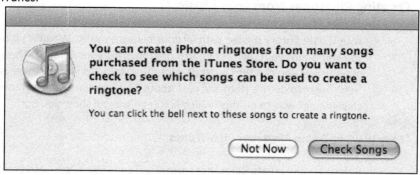

You can create iPhone ringtones from many songs purchased from the iTunes Store. Do you want to check to see which songs can be used to create a ringtone?

You can click the bell next to these songs to create a ringtone.

Not Now   Check Songs

Select **"Check Songs"** and iTunes will begin to arrange your music and show you which songs can be turned into "Ringtones."

CHARGE FOR RINGTONE CREATION: Be aware that iTunes charges for this service, usually US $0.99 for each Ringtone created.

Next, Open up your iTunes "Preferences" menu, as shown on page 62.

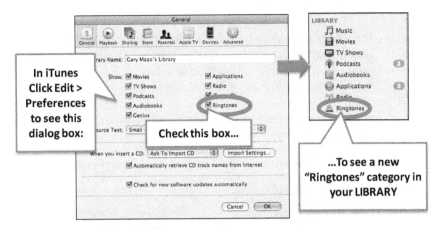

In iTunes Click Edit > Preferences to see this dialog box:

Check this box...

...To see a new "Ringtones" category in your LIBRARY

Make sure that you have "Ringtones" checked in this screen as well so you will be able to see your Ringtones from the left hand menu pane in iTunes.

Choose the Song from Which to Create a Ringtone

Now we are ready to choose a song from which we will make a Ringtone. Just make sure that you see the little ringtone icon next to the song in iTunes in the new "Ringtone" column.

Highlight the song, then select **"Store"** > **"Create Ringtone"** from the menu. iTunes will change to show you the "Create Ringtone" page.

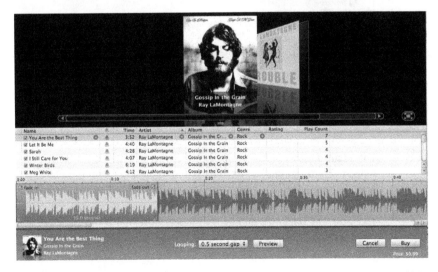

The song is displayed as a "Sound wave" along the bottom with the first 15 seconds highlighted in Blue. You can grab the blue highlighted section in the middle and "drag" it to any section of the song. You can also drag either of the corners to extend the ringtone beyond the initial 15 seconds.

In this example, I have highlighted the section I want of a particular song to almost 30 seconds.

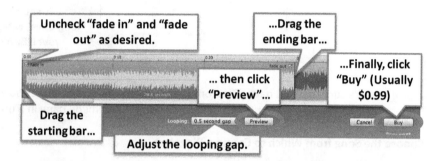

To listen to the highlighted section, just click on **"Preview."** When you are satisfied with the selection, select **"Buy"** and input your iTunes password if prompted.

Once your purchase the Ringtone, it will appear in the "Ringtone" list. Just click on "Ringtones" in the left hand pane of iTunes.

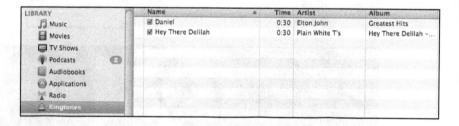

"More Challenging Way" to Create Ring Tones – Manual Creation (It's FREE)

The second method for creating a Ringtone is a little trickier. It certainly helps to be "technically inclined" if you are going to try this method. One very good reason to try this method is that it is totally free.

This method will work on any music in iTunes that is not protected with DRM (Digital Rights Management) copy protection. Older iTunes purchases might contain DRM. Any music you loaded into iTunes from a CD or other non DRM music (including newer non-DRM music from iTunes) will work.

Locate the Song to Turn into Your Custom Ringtone

First, we need to locate the song in our iTunes library – a simple search will locate the song. Learn all about the iTunes "Search" on page 63.

Once the song is found, click on it to highlight it.

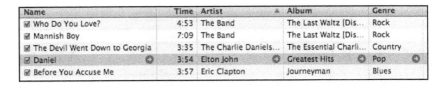

Name	Time	Artist		Album		Genre	
☑ Who Do You Love?	4:53	The Band		The Last Waltz [Dis...		Rock	
☑ Mannish Boy	7:09	The Band		The Last Waltz [Dis...		Rock	
☑ The Devil Went Down to Georgia	3:35	The Charlie Daniels...		The Essential Charli...		Country	
☑ Daniel	3:54	Elton John		Greatest Hits		Pop	
☑ Before You Accuse Me	3:57	Eric Clapton		Journeyman		Blues	

In the iTunes menu, go up to the "**File**" menu and then click on **"Get info."** You can also "Right Click" the mouse and choose "Get info."

Move over to the "Options" tab and put a check mark in the "Start time" and "Stop Time" boxes. WARNING: Make sure the total duration is less than 40 seconds, otherwise the Ringtone will be too large.

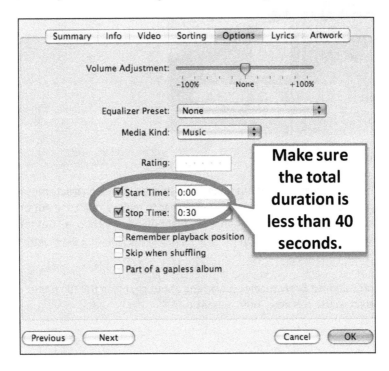

Next, click "OK" to return to the list of songs.

Highlight the song we edited for Start/Stop time and go to the "Advanced" menu and select "Create ACC Version." (TIP: You should also be able to right-click the song and select it from the drop down list.) iTunes will then covert the selection to the proper format and create a new song of the duration specified below the original as shown.

☑ Daniel	⟳	3:54
☑ Daniel		0:30

Once you have your new 30 second version, make sure you go back into the "Get Info" > "Options" tab and uncheck the start/end times so that your original song will play in its entirety.

Once the new, 30 second ACC version of the song is created, just "drag" it from iTunes to your desktop – or you can "Copy" it and "Paste" it to the desktop as well.

Change the Name of the File

The file we just created has a file extension (the last 3 characters of the file name) of "m4a." We need to change that to make a ring tone out of it. Click on the file to highlight the name or "Right Click" and choose **"Get Info"** and then change the extension to "m4r" – this is the ringtone extension needed for the iPhone.

You will most likely receive a warning about changing the file name – just select to use the new "m4r" extension.

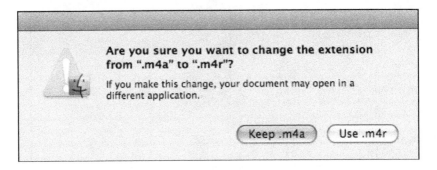

KEY STEP: Before moving onto the next step, go back into iTunes and **delete** the 30 second version of the song that you just converted into a ringtone. ITunes will not let you proceed with the next step until that file is deleted.

Move the new Ringtone File Back into iTunes

Once the new file is created and the 0:30 second file in iTunes has been deleted, drag the new ".m4r" file back into iTunes (or use Copy and Paste if you are more comfortable). Place it in the "Ringtones" folder – just drag it to the "Ringtones" icon or click on "Ringtones" in the left hand pane and select "Paste."

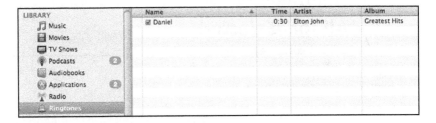

You should now see the new ringtone you just created in the ringtone folder.

Syncing the Ringtone to your iPhone

In iTunes, click on your iPhone under "**DEVICES**" to highlight it.
Then, click on the "Ringtones" tab in the main window in iTunes.

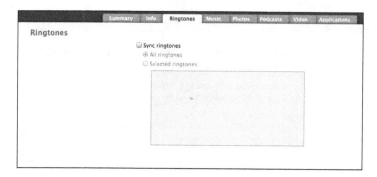

You should now see our new "Ringtone" (Daniel) that we just made. Click the box for "Sync Ringtones" and either choose to sync just the one ringtone or all the ones that you purchase or create.

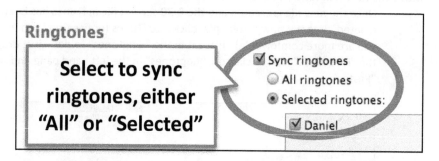

Using your New Custom Ringtone

If you want to tie your ringtone to a particular person in your Address Book, then follow the steps on page 122.

If you want to use your new ringtone for your main phone ringtone, then see the steps on page 121.

Chapter 6:
Your iPhone Camera

Your iPhone comes with a 2.0 Mega Pixel camera. It is easy to take pictures, file them and send them (via email) to your contacts.

Starting the Camera App

The "**Camera**" icon should be on your home page – usually on the first screen at the top. If you don't see it, then flip left or right until you find it.

Touch the "**Camera**" icon and the shutter of the camera opens with an animation on your screen.

Geo-Tagging

Geo-Tagging is a feature that puts your geographical GPS (Geographic Positioning System) coordinates into the picture file. If you upload your pictures to programs like "Flickr," the coordinates of your picture can be used for your friends to locate you and locate the site of where the picture was taken.

If you have "Location Services" turned on (see page 295) when you start the camera, you will be asked if it is OK to use your current location.

You have the option of saying "**OK**" or "**Don't Allow.**" You need to select "**OK**" for Geo-tagging to work.

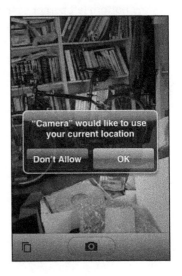

Taking a Picture

Once your camera is on, center your subject in the screen of your iPhone.

Can I Zoom In?
No. As of publishing time, the iPhone did not allow you to zoom in.

When you are ready to take a picture, just touch the "**Camera**" button along the bottom. You will hear a shutter sound and the screen will show an animation indicating that the picture is being taken.

Once the picture is taken, you will see the picture on the screen.

Viewing Pictures you have Taken

Your iPhone will store pictures you take on the iPhone in what is called your "Camera Roll." You can access the Camera Roll from inside both the Camera and Pictures icons. In the Camera, touch the "pictures" icon in the bottom left corner of the camera screen.

Once you touch a picture to view, you can "Swipe" through you pictures like we showed you on page 26.

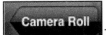To get back to the Camera Roll, press the Camera Roll button in the upper left corner.

To take another picture, touch the camera icon in the upper right corner.

Viewing from "Photos" Icon

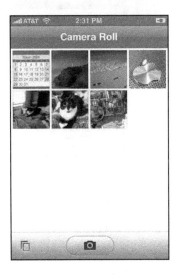

You can also view the pictures taken by your camera in your "Photos" Icon.

Tap the Photo Icon (see page 269 for help) and you will see a new Photo Album called **"Camera Roll."** Once you tap Camera Roll, you will see all the pictures you have taken.

Tap any picture to view it.
Remember the "Pinch Open" and "Pinch Closed" finger motions to zoom in and zoom out of your pictures (see page 29)

Deleting a Picture from the Camera Roll

Deleting a picture from the "Camera Roll" is just like deleting a picture for any Photo album. Just touch any picture from your Camera Roll and then touch the small "Trash Can" icon at the bottom right of the screen. Confirm the "Delete" and the photo will be deleted from the screen.

Transferring Pictures to Your Computer

You can always email pictures one at a time from your iPhone to your computer, but it is not practical when you want to get lots of pictures quickly from your iPhone to your computer.

Apple Mac users will be able to transfer photos to iPhoto when you connect your iPhone to your Mac. You will see iPhoto open up automatically and show you the photos and images stored on your iPhone. You can then decide what to copy to your Mac and what to copy to your iPhone.

Windows PC users will need to browse to the computer from the Start Menu. Windows Logo > Computer or Start Menu > My Computer to see all disk drives and connected icons. You should see an icon for your iPhone as shown below:

The next step is to continue double-clicking on the iPhone and folders contained inside it until you see the images from the iPhone. The number of times you need to double-click and the specific folder names may vary a bit, but keep double-clicking until you see the images/photos.

On our iPhone in this book we double-clicked on the iPhone icon to open it up and see "Internal Storage." Then, we double-clicked on "Internal Storage" to see a folder labeled "DCIM." We double-clicked again on the "DCIM" folder to see another folder (ours was called "100APPLE".) Finally, when we opened this folder, we saw all the images stored on our iPhone as shown below.

Now that we can see the images and photos on our iPhone, we need to copy them from our iPhone to our computer. To do this we select one or all using the selection and copy or "drag and drop" methods shown on page 84 (In the manually managing music iTunes section).

Emailing a Photo, Assigning to a Contact, Use as Wallpaper

 With every picture you have, you can do many things with it. Tap this icon in the lower left corner when you are viewing the picture to use it as Wallpaper, Email a Photo, Assign to Contact and send as MMS(new in 3.0 software)
EMAIL A PHOTO: See page 274.
USE PHOTO AS WALLPAPER: See page 163
ASSIGN PHOTO TO CONTACT: See on page 274.

New 3.0 Feature: Send Picture via MMS

 The iPhone software version 3.0 adds MMS (Multi-Media Messaging) as an option for sending pictures.
This allows your picture to be sent inside the body of the message and can be delivered to mobile phones that sometimes cannot receive email messages.

Look on page 136 to read all about it!

Chapter 7:
Bluetooth on the iPhone

The iPhone ships with Bluetooth 2.0 Technology. Think of Bluetooth as a short range, wireless technology which allows your iPhone to "connect" to various peripheral devices without wires. Popular devices are headsets, computers, and vehicle sound systems.

Bluetooth is believed to be named after a Danish Viking and King, Harald Blåtand (which has been translated as *Bluetooth* in English.) King Blåtand lived in the 10th century and is famous for uniting Denmark and Norway. Similarly, Bluetooth technology unites computers and telecom. His name, according to legend, is from his very dark hair which was unusual for Vikings. Blåtand means dark complexion. There does exist a more popular story which states that the King loved to eat Blueberries, so much so his teeth became stained with the color Blue.

Sources:
http://cp.literature.agilent.com/litweb/pdf/5980-3032EN.pdf
http://www.cs.utk.edu/~dasgupta/bluetooth/history.htm
http://www.britannica.com/eb/topic-254809/Harald-I

Understanding Bluetooth

Bluetooth allows your iPhone to communicate with things like headsets, GPS devices and other hands-free systems with the freedom of wireless. Bluetooth is a small radio that transmits from each device. The iPhone gets "paired" – connected to the peripheral. Many Bluetooth devices can be used up to 30 feet away from the iPhone.

Bluetooth Devices that work with the iPhone

The iPhone 3G works with Bluetooth headsets, hands free car kits and Bluetooth Speakerphones. The new software upgrade (version 3.0) supports A2DP – which is known as "Stereo Bluetooth." We cover this in the chapter on the 3.0 upgrade on page 232.

Once you upgrade to version 3.0 you will be able to use your iPhone to play music using Bluetooth stereo headphones or a Bluetooth stereo system in your car or in your home.

Pairing with (Connecting to) a Bluetooth Headset

Your primary use for Bluetooth will most likely be with a Bluetooth headset for "Hands free" calling. Any Bluetooth headset should work well with your iPhone. To start using any Bluetooth device, you need to first "pair" it with your iPhone.

Turn "ON" Bluetooth

The first step to using Bluetooth is to turn the Bluetooth Radio "ON."

Tap your "**Settings**" icon , then, touch the "**General**" tab

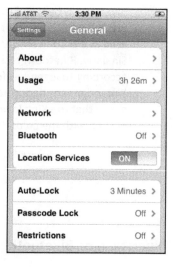

and scroll down to "Bluetooth."

By default, Bluetooth is initially "**OFF**" on the iPhone. Tap the switch to move it to the "**ON**" position. Once turned on, the iPhone will immediately start searching for Bluetooth devices in range.

BATTERY SAVING TIP: Bluetooth is an added drain to your battery. If you don't plan on using Bluetooth for a period of time, think about turning the switch back to "Off."

Pairing with a Headset or any Bluetooth Device

As soon as you turn Bluetooth "**ON**," the iPhone will begin to search for any nearby Bluetooth device – like a Bluetooth headset. Put your headset into "Pairing mode." Read the instructions carefully that came with your headset – usually there is a combination of buttons to push to achieve this. TIP: Some headsets require you to press and hold a button for 5 seconds until you see a flashing blue or red/blue lights.

Once the iPhone detects the headset, it will attempt to "automatically" pair with the headset. If paring takes place automatically, there is nothing more for you to do.

If the iPhone asks for a "PIN" or "Pass code" to be entered, the keyboard will be displayed and you enter the four digit pass code supplied by the headset manufacturer. Most headsets use 0000 or 1234 which is why the iPhone can try to automatically pair with most headsets. Check your headset documentation to learn the correct pass code or PIN for your device.

Using the Bluetooth Headset

If your headset it properly "Paired" and "ON," all incoming calls should be routed to your headset. Usually you can just press the main button on the headset to answer the call or use the "Slide to Answer" function on the iPhone.

Move the phone away from your face (while the iPhone is dialing) and you should see the indicator showing you that the Bluetooth headset is in use. In the image you see that the speaker icon is next to the "Jawbone" Bluetooth headset.

You will also see the options to send the call to your iPhone handset or to the **"Speaker phone."** You can change this at any point while you are on the call.

Options when On a Call

Once the call is made and you are speaking with your contact, you can still re-route the call to either the iPhone or the Speakerphone.

Move the call away from your face (if it is near your face) and you will see

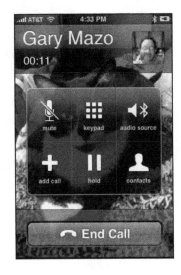

"Audio Source" as one of the options for you to touch. Touch that icon and you will have all the options for re-routing the call as shown above.

Just choose to send the call to any of the options shown and you will see the small speaker icon move to the current source being used for the call.

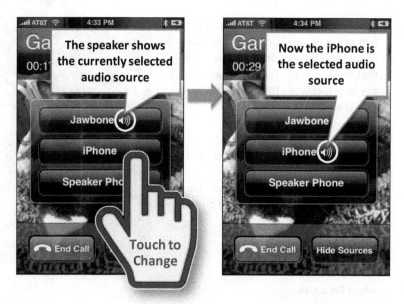

Bluetooth Stereo (A2DP) - New in Version 3.0

 One of the great features of today's advanced Bluetooth technology is the ability to "stream" your music without wires via Bluetooth. The fancy name for this technology is A2DP, but it is simply known as "Stereo Bluetooth." Now, for this first time, this feature is available on iPhone with 3.0 software.

Connect to a Stereo Bluetooth Device

The first step to using Stereo Bluetooth is to connect to a capable Stereo Bluetooth device. This can be a Car Stereo with this technology built in or a pair of Bluetooth Headphones or speakers.

Put the Bluetooth device into "Pairing" mode as per the manufacturer's instructions and then go to the Bluetooth setting page from the Settings icon as we show you on Page 138.

Once connected, you will see the new Stereo Bluetooth device listed under your Bluetooth devices.

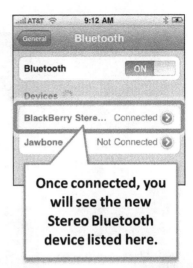

Once connected, you will see the new Stereo Bluetooth device listed here.

Next, tap your iPod icon and start up any song, playlist, podcast or video Music library. You will now notice a small Bluetooth icon in the lower right hand corner of the screen. Tap the Bluetooth icon to see the available Bluetooth devices for "Streaming" your music.

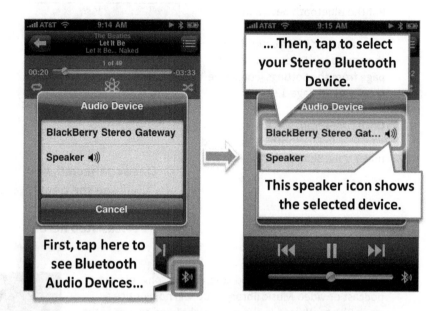

In the above screens, we selected the "BlackBerry Stereo Gateway" by tapping it. Now, your music will now start to play from the selected Bluetooth device. You can verify this again by touching the Bluetooth icon on the screen once more. You should see the "**Speaker**" icon next to the new Stereo Bluetooth device and you should hear your music coming from that sound source as well.

Chapter 8:
SMS Text and
MMS Multi-Media Messaging

SMS stands for Short Messaging Service and it is commonly referred to as "Text Messaging." Text messages are usually limited to 160 characters and are a great way to quickly touch base with someone without interrupting them with a voice call. Sometimes you can text someone and receive a text reply when it would be impossible or difficult to do a voice call.

SMS Text Messaging on your iPhone

Text messaging has become one of the most popular services on cell phones today. While it is still used more extensively in Europe and Asia, it is growing in popularity in North America.

The concept is very simple; instead of placing a phone call – send a short message to someone's handset. It is much less disruptive than a phone call and you may have friends, colleagues or co-workers who do not own an iPhone – so email may not be an option.

One of the authors uses text messaging with his children all the time – this is how their generation communicates. "R u coming home 4 dinner?" "Yup." There you have it – meaningful dialogue with a seventeen year old – short, instant and easy.

New 3.0 OS Option: Messages Icon

In the new version 3.0 operating system, the SMS icon will be replaced by a "Messages" icon. Users can now sending pictures and audio via MMS messaging. Look on page 136 for all the details.

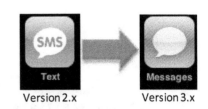

Version 2.x   Version 3.x

Composing SMS Text Messages

Composing an SMS message is much like sending an email. The beauty of an SMS message is that it arrives on virtually any handset and is quite simple to reply.

Composing an SMS Message from the SMS icon or Messaging

There are a couple of ways to start your SMS messaging App. The easiest is to just touch the SMS Icon (if you have a 2.x iPhone) or touch the Messaging Icon (if you have version 3.0 and higher of the iPhone Software) on the home screen.

When you first start the SMS App you most likely won't have any messages, so the screen will be blank. Once you get started with SMS messaging you will have a list of messages and current "open" discussions with your contacts.

Touch the "Compose" icon in the top right hand corner of the screen.

The cursor will immediately go to the "To" line. You can either start typing in the name of your contact or just touch the "+" button and search or scroll through your contacts.

If you want to just type someone's mobile phone number, then press the "123" button and dial the number.

When you find the contact you wish to use, just touch the name and now their name will appear in the "To:" line.

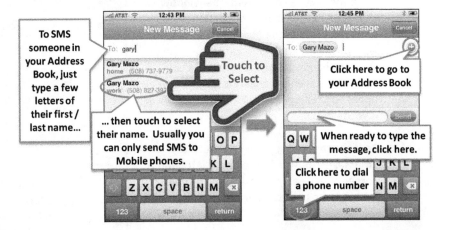

When you are ready to type the SMS message, touch anywhere in the box in the middle of the screen (next to the "**Send**" button).

The keyboard will be displayed. Just type in your message and then touch "**Send**" when you are done.

New in 3.0: If you prefer, you can use the larger landscape keyboard for sending Text Messages. It can be easier to type with the larger keys, especially when your fingers are a little larger, or it is hard to see the smaller keys.

Options after sending a text

Once the text has been sent, the window changes to a "threaded" discussion window between you and the contact. Your text that you sent is in Green text in a bubble on the right hand side of the screen. When your contact replies, their message will appear on the opposite side of the screen in a White bubble.

To leave the SMS screen, just touch the "**Messages**" button in the upper left hand corner or you can just touch the "**Home**" button to go back to your home screen.

You can send another text just as you did before or you can also "Call" the contact or view their "Contact info."

To initiate a call to the contact with whom you are "texting" just touch the "**Call**" button. To look at their contact info, just touch the **"Contact Info"** button.

Composing an SMS Message from "Contacts"

You also have the message to start the SMS App and compose an SMS message from any contact in your iPhone.

Just find the contact you wish to "text" by searching or scrolling through "Contacts."

At the very bottom of the contact info there will be a box that says "Text Message." Just touch that box and you will be prompted to choose which number to use (if you have more than one number listed for the contact.)

NOTE: Remember that you can only send SMS messages to a mobile number.

Choose the number and follow the steps above.

Replying to a Text Message

When Text message is received, your iPhone will play an indicator tone or vibrate or both – depending on your settings. An indicator will appear on the screen giving you the option of replying right away.

When you see and/or hear the indicator, just touch "**Reply**" to go directly to the messaging screen and type your response as you did above.

Viewing Stored Messages

Once you begin a few threaded messages, they will be stored in the SMS Icon. Just touch the SMS icon and you can scroll through your message threads.

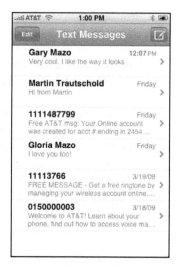

To continue a conversation with someone, just touch on that "thread" and it will open up showing you all the past messages back and forth. Just touch the text box, type in your message and touch the "**Send**" button to continue the conversation.

SMS Notification Options

There are a couple of options available to you with regards to how your iPhone reacts when an SMS message comes in.

Start your "**Settings**" App and scroll to "**Sounds**" and touch the tab. In the sound menu, if you choose to have the "**Vibrate**" feature on when the phone rings (see page 121) you will also receive a vibration when an SMS message comes in.

Scroll down a bit further and you will see a tab that says "**New Text Message.**" Touch this and you can choose the tone for the SMS message. You are limited to the choices offered (usually 6) or you can choose "none."

Just choose the sound for SMS message notification and then touch the "**Sounds**"

button in the top left hand corner to "set" your selection.

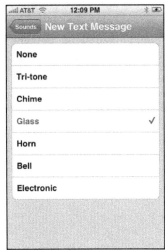

MMS

With 3.0 software, iPhone users have the tools to send and receive Multi-Media Messages – including picture messages and voice memo messages. MMS messages appear right in the messaging window like your SMS text messages.

SOME CARRIERS DO NOT SUPPORT MMS: As of publishing time, AT&T in the USA had not yet fully implemented MMS. This may change by the time you read this book. Check with your carrier to see if you can send or receive MMS (Multi-Media Messages) directly from your iPhone.

The "Messages" Icon

On version 3.0 software, the "SMS" icon has been replaced with a "Messages" icon. Touch the "Messages" icon to start messaging – just like you did with SMS.

The Text enter screen is the same as in the SMS program covered on Page 146. You will notice that next to the Text input bubble is a small "Camera" image. Just touch the camera and you will be prompted to **"Take a Photo"** or **"Choose an Existing"** Photo.

To take a photo, follow the instructions on Page 132. If you **"Choose Existing"** photo, just navigate through your pictures and find the picture you would like to add to your message.

Touch the blue "**Choose**" button in the lower right hand corner and you will see the picture load into the small window.

Select a the recipient as you did on Page 146 and type in a short note if you like. Then, touch the blue "**Send**" button.

If you already have a threaded discussion with that particular contact, the picture will show up in the midst of the threaded discussion.

Choosing a Picture from "Photos" to Send via MMS

The second way to send an MMS message is to just go straight to your "Photos" App and choose a picture.

Start your "Photos" App and navigate your pictures as you did on Page 269. To only send ONE picture, just touch the picture you wish to send and then touch the "send" icon in the lower left hand corner. You will now see MMS as the second option.

Choose MMS and the photo will load into the "Bubble" just as above.

To Send Multiple Pictures

Start up your "**Photos**" App as you did above. Instead of touching one picture, touch the "**Send**" icon in the lower left hand corner. Now, just tap as many pictures as you want. You will see then lighten in color and then a red check mark appears in the box.

Once you have all the picture chosen, just touch the "**Share**" button in the lower left hand corner. Choose "**MMS**" and the pictures will appear in the Messaging window.

Chapter 9:
Moving, Docking, and Deleting Icons

Your iPhone is very customizable; you can move icons around, have your favorite four icons located in the bottom dock and adjust the look and feel so it suits your tastes. Similar to an Apple Mac computer, there is a Bottom Dock where you can put your favorite icons.

Moving Icons to the Bottom Dock - "Docking Them"

When you turn your iPhone on, you will notice that there are four icons "locked" on the bottom dock. The "Standard" four icons locked to the bottom dock are: "Phone," "Mail," "Safari," (web browser) and "iPod."

Now, you might decide that you wish to change one or more of these to an App that you use more often. Fortunately, moving icons to the bottom dock is easy.

Keep up to 4 icons that you want to see all the time. These icons will always remain visible even when you slide the other icon screens left/right.

Bottom Dock

Starting the Move
Press the "Home" button and get to your Home Screen of icons. Now, touch and hold any icon on the home screen for a couple of seconds. You will notice that all the icons start to shake.

Just try moving a couple of icons around at first. You will notice that when you move an icon down, the other icons in the row will move to make space for it.

Once you have the feel for how the icons move, you are ready to replace one of the "Bottom Dock" icons. While the icons are shaking, take the icon you wish to replace from the bottom dock and move it up to the main screen.

NOTE: You can only have 4 icons in the Bottom Dock, so if you already have 4 there, then you will have to remove one to replace it with a new one.

What I want to do is replace the "**iTunes**" icon with my "**Safari**" icon, so the first thing I do is just hold and move the iTunes icon up a row – out of the bottom dock.

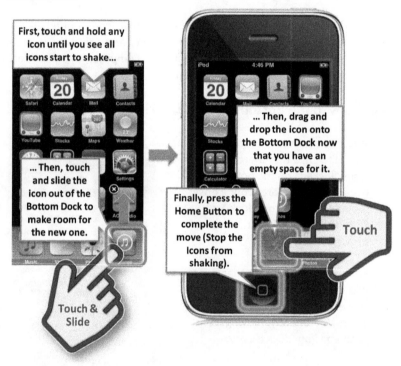

Next, I locate my Safari icon and move it down to the bottom dock – notice that it is sort of transparent until I actually "set" it into place.

When I am sure that I have it just where I want it, I simply press the "Home" key once and the icons "set" and "lock" into place. Now, I have my Browser in the bottom dock where I want it.

Moving Icons to a Different Icon Page

Your iPhone puts 16 icons on a "page" and these pages can be found by just "Swiping" (right to left) on your home screen. With all the cool Apps available, it is not uncommon to have five, six or even more pages full with icons.

Sometimes, there is an icon you rarely use that may be on your first page and you want to move it way off to the end page. This is very easy to do and is handled in a very similar fashion to the "moving" icons to the Bottom Dock discussed above.

Touch and Hold any icon to initiate the "Moving"

Touch and hold the icon you wish to move. In the images that follow, we want to move my "Stocks" image to the last page – it is just too depressing to look at these days!

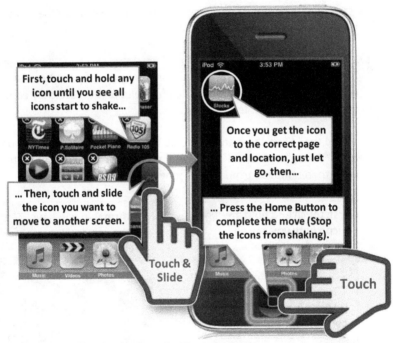

Then, Drag and Drop the Icon On To another Page
I Touch and hold the "**Stocks**" icon and drag it to the right. I will see all my pages of icons move by and when I get to the last page, I just "release" the icon and it is now placed at the very end.

Press the Home Key to Complete the move and stop the Icons from shaking.

Deleting Icons

It is as easy to delete an icon as it is to move it. One thing to remember, however, is that when an Icon is deleted, we are actually deleting the program from our iPhone. This means you won't be able to use the Icon again without re-installing or re-downloading it.

Depending on my Sync settings in iTunes, the program may still reside in my "Applications" in iTunes and I can re-install it at another time if I like.

Touch and Hold any Icon to Initiate "Deleting"

Just as we did before, "Touching" and "Holding" will make the icons "shake" and allow us to move and delete them.

NOTE: You can only delete icons (programs) that you have downloaded to your iPhone – the pre-installed icons and programs cannot be deleted. You can tell which programs are available for deletion because they contain a small "x" in the upper left hand corner.

Just tap the "x" on the icon you would like to delete. You will be prompted to either "Delete" or "Cancel" the delete request. If you select "Delete," the icon is then removed from your iPhone.

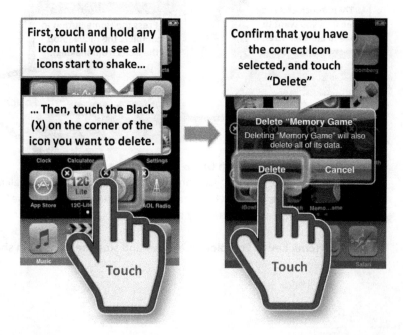

160

Resetting All Your Icon Locations (Factory Defaults)

Occasionally, you might want to get back to the original or 'Factory Default' icon settings.   An example of when you might want to do this is when you have moved too many new Icons to your first page and want to see all the 'basic' iPhone icons again.

To do this, touch the Settings Icon. Then touch **"General"** and finally scroll all the way to the bottom to touch **"Reset."**

On the Reset screen, touch "Reset Home Screen Layout" near the bottom. Now all your Icons will be returned to the original default settings.

Chapter 10:
Personalize your iPhone

In this chapter you will learn some great ways to personalize your iPhone. You can change everything from your "Wallpaper" to sounds and more. Many things can be fine-tuned to meet your needs and tastes -- to give your iPhone a more "personal" look and feel.

Changing your Wallpaper

When you first turn on your iPhone or "wake" it up, you will see your "wallpaper" behind the "Slide to Unlock" button. You will also see your wallpaper behind the phone when you are in a call. When you first turn on your iPhone, you might not have any wallpaper set or it might be just black with the clock.

There are a couple of ways to change your wallpaper on the iPhone. The first way is very straightforward.

Changing Wallpaper from the Settings icon

Touch the "Settings" icon then touch the "Wallpaper" tab and you will see a screen showing you the Wallpaper folder, the Camera Roll (if you have taken pictures with your iPhone) and folders for your photo library and any other libraries you might have synced in iTunes.

Touch any of the Albums displayed, or tap the "**Wallpaper**" tab to see all the pre-loaded wallpapers for the iPhone. Tap the picture that you desire and a preview screen will appear.

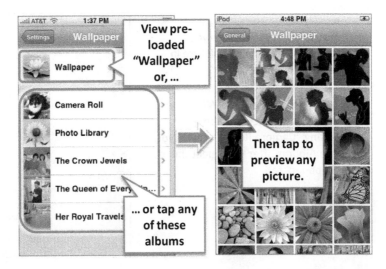

If you wish to select the picture shown as your wallpaper, touch **"Set Wallpaper."**

If you don't want to use that picture, choose "**Cancel**" and you will return to the page of thumbnails to choose another picture.

Change Wallpaper from any Picture

The second way to change your wallpaper is to view any picture in your "Photos" collection.

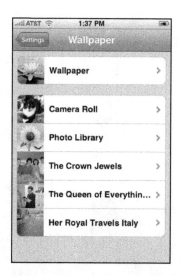

You can do this from the Wallpaper tab which we described above by selecting "Camera Roll" or any of your Photo Albums after you select the "Wallpaper" tab.

You can also touch your "Photos" icon and you will also see your picture albums.

Touch the Photo album you with to look through. When you find a photo that will work for you, just "Touch" it and it will open in your screen.

At the bottom left hand corner of the photo is the "Set as" icon. Just touch that icon and three options pop up on the screen, the first one being "Use As Wallpaper."

If you are sure that you wish to use that picture as your wallpaper, touch on the "**Use as Wallpaper**" button. The next screen is called the "Move and Scale" screen. Here, if you touch the "**Set Wallpaper**" button, the picture will be properly scaled for your screen.

If you decide you wish to use a different picture, choose "**Cancel**" and pick a different one.

Keyboard Options & Settings

You can fine-tune your keyboard by selecting various languages, and changing settings like "Auto-Correction" and "Auto-Capitalization." See page 54 in our Typing Tips chapter for keyboard options and how to use the various features.

Security Options

Your iPhone can hold a great deal of your valuable information. This is especially true if you save information like Social Security Numbers and Birth Dates of your family members. It is a good idea to make sure that someone who picks up your iPhone can't access all your information. Also, if your kids are like ours, they might just pick up your cool iPhone and start surfing the web. You might want to enable some security restrictions to keep them safe.

Setting a Passcode -- a Password to Lock Your iPhone

Touch the "Settings" icon and then the "General" tab. Now scroll down to tap on the "Passcode Lock" item.

You have the option of setting a four digit "Passcode" to get into your iPhone and your information. If the wrong Passcode is input, you can't access your information – so it is a good idea to use a code that you will easily remember.

Use the Keypad and key in a four digit code. You will then be prompted to enter your code once more.

TIP: Once you have set your Passcode, the next time you enter the Passcode Lock screen, you will be presented with a few options:
"Turn Passcode Off"
"Change Passcode"
"Require Passcode" (Immediately, 1 min., 5 min., 15 min., 1 hour, 4 hours) NOTE: Setting a shorter time will be a more secure setting.
"Erase Data" (Default is "OFF" - if set to "ON" this will erase all data after 10 unsuccessful attempts to enter your passcode.

You will then be taken to the "Passcode Lock" screen where you can turn off the passcode feature, change your passcode and change the "Require Passcode" time from "Immediately" to any other time period you desire.

To make changes in these settings (like turning the passcode off) you will be prompted again to enter your code.

Setting Restrictions

You might decide that you don't want your kids listening to "Explicit" lyrics in music that may be on your iPhone. You might also not want them to visit YouTube and seeing content you find objectionable. Setting these restrictions is quite easy on your iPhone.

Once again, Touch the "General" tab under "Settings" and this time, scroll down to "Restrictions" and touch.

You will see a large button that says "Enable Restrictions."

When you Touch this, you will be prompted to enter a "Restrictions" Passcode – just pick a four-digit code you will remember.

You will need to enter this Restriction Passcode to turn off restrictions later.

Enter your code and then you can adjust the sliders for "Explicit" music, "Safari" web sites, "YouTube," iTunes" and "Installing Apps."

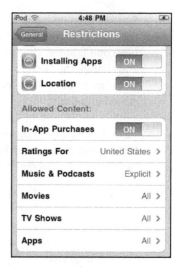

OFF = RESTRICTED
You might think that "ON" is restricted, but it is the opposite -- In order to disable or restrict something, you need to touch the slider next to it and change it to "OFF." If you look at the word "Allow:" above all the tabs, then it makes sense.

You can see here that I have restricted access to "Explicit" lyrics and "YouTube."

Chapter 11:
Playing Music (iPod)

Your iPhone as a Music Player

Your iPhone is such a capable device that you might forget that it is also the best portable music player on the market today. Your iPhone plays, organizes, randomizes and allows you to view, listen and customize pretty much every aspect of your music. And, with new 3.0 software, you can even "Shake to Shuffle" - see how on page 182.

Music and Video on the iPhone

Music and Video on the iPhone (as opposed to the iPod Touch) are handled through the "iPod" icon on the home screen.

Touch the iPod icon and there are four "Soft Keys" across the bottom:
Playlists - See all your playlists
Artists - See an alphabetical list of artists (searchable like your Address Book)
Songs - See an alphabetical list of songs (also searchable)
Videos - See an alphabetical list of videos (also searchable)

To see the "Album" view of your music, just touch the "More" soft key and you will see "Albums" at the top of the list.

"Editing" the Soft Keys

One very cool feature on the iPhone is that you can "Edit" the soft keys at the bottom of the "iPod" App and really customize it to fit your needs and tastes.

Just touch the "Edit" button at the top left of the screen.

The screen changes to show you the various icons that can be "Dragged" down to the bottom dock.

Let's say you wanted to replace the "Videos" icons with one for "Albums." Just touch and hold the "Albums" icon and drag it to the spot where the

Visit us at www.MadeSimpleLearning.com

"Video" icon is. When you get to the bottom dock, just release the icon and the "Albums" icon will now reside where the "Videos" icon was. You can do this with any of the icons in this "Configure" screen. When you are done, just touch the "Done" icon at the top right of the screen.

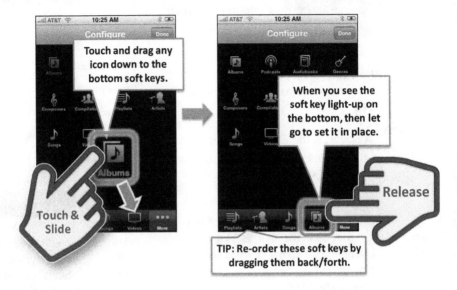

TIP: You can also re-order the icons across the bottom by dragging and dropping them back or forth along the soft key row.

Playlists View

Playlists are created in iTunes on your computer and then Synced to your iPhone.

How can I create a Playlist?
Learn how to create playlists on page 171.

A playlist is something you create and can be made up of a particular genre, artist, year of recording or any collection of songs that interest you.

Once a playlist is synced to your iPhone, it shows up in the "Playlist" view. In this example, I touch my "Classic Rock" playlist and all the songs from that playlist are listed.

NOTE: You can edit the contents of your Playlists on your iPhone, but not create new ones. To create a new Playlist, do it in iTunes on your Computer (see page 68).

To go to a different Playlist, I just touch the "Playlist" tab at the top of the screen.

Searching For Music

In almost every view in your iPod Icon (Playlists, Artists, Videos, Songs, etc.) if you flick your finger down to bring yourself to above the first item shown on the screen, you will then see a "Search" window. Just tap once in that search window and start typing a few letters of the name of your Artist, Playlist, Video or Song to instantly see a list of all matching items. This is the best way to find something to listen to or watch quickly on your iPhone.

Artists View

The "Artists" view will list all the artists on your iPhone. Just "Flick" through the list to advance to the first letter of the artist's name you are looking for. Once you find the Artist's name, just touch that name and all the songs by that artist will be listed with a picture of the album art to the left.

TIP: Use the same navigation and searching features as you do with your Contacts Icon (Address Book).

Songs View

Touching the "Songs" tab will show you a listing of every song on your iPhone. If you know the exact name of the song you desire, just flick through the list or touch the first letter of the song in the alphabetical list to the right.

Albums View

Your iPhone can also organize your music by Albums when you Touch the "Albums" tab at the bottom. Again, you can "Flick" through the list or touch the first letter of the album name you are looking for in the alphabetical list and then make your selection. Once you choose an album, all the songs on that album will be listed.

More Viewing Options

If you Touch the "More" tab to the bottom right, you will then see tabs for "Audiobooks," "Compilations," "Composers," Genres" and "Podcasts. Just Touch the selection you desire and you can see your music organized by those categories.

Navigating with "Cover Flow" View

"Cover Flow" is the proprietary and very cool manner of looking at your music by album covers. When you are playing a song in the iPod Music icon and simply turn your iPhone horizontal – into "Landscape" mode, your iPhone will automatically change to "Cover Flow" view.

Touch the cover and flick left or right to go to another Album.

Touch & Flick Left/Right

Touch here to play or pause the song.

Touch here view a list of songs from this Album.

In Cover Flow view, you just use your finger and "Swipe" through the Album Art until you see the artist or album you are looking for. It doesn't matter if you are in "Playlists," "Albums" or any other sub-section of your Music Player – when you turn your iPhone horizontal, you will change to "Cover Flow" view.

Viewing Songs In Cover Flow

Just touch an Album Cover and the cover will "Flip" showing you the songs on that particular album.

To see the song that is playing now (in CoverFlow view) just tap the album cover and it will "turn over" revealing all the songs on that album. The song that is "playing now" will have a small blue arrow next to it.

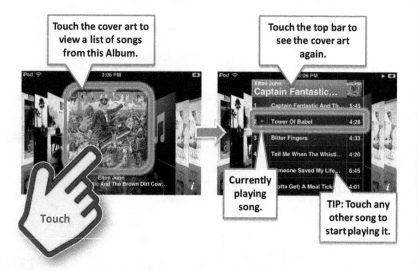

Tap the title bar (above the list of songs) and the Album Cover will be displayed once more. You can then keep "Swiping" through your music until you find what you are searching for.

NOTE: You can also touch the small "*i*" that is in the lower right hand corner and the album cover will "flip" showing you the songs, just as if you touched the cover.

Playing your Music

Now that you know how to "find" your music, it is time to "Play" it. If your iPhone is Vertical and you have found your song (either the beginning of a playlist or an individual song) just touch the song name and it will begin to play.

The screen shows a picture of the Album from which the song originates and the name of the song at the top.

Along the bottom is the "Volume Bar," "Play/Pause" Key and the "Next" and "Previous" Buttons.

Pausing and Playing

Just touch the "Pause" symbol (if your song is playing) or the "Play" arrow (if the music is paused) to play or resume your song.

To play the "Previous" or "Next" song

If you are in a "Playlist," touching the "Next" arrow (to the right of the Play/Pause button) will advance you to the "Next" song in the list. If you are searching through your music by "Album," touching next will advance to the next song on the album. Touching the "Previous" button will do just the reverse.

Adjusting the Volume

There are two ways to adjust the volume on your iPhone: using the external volume buttons or using the volume slider control on the screen.

The external volume buttons are on the upper left hand side of the device – just press the "Volume Up" key (top of the two) or the "Volume Down" key to raise or lower the volume key. You will see the Volume slider control move as you adjust the volume. You can also just Touch and hold the volume slider key and adjust the volume up or down.

Double-Click Home Button for iPod Controls

You can play your music while you are doing other things on your iPhone - like reading and responding to email, playing a game, browsing the web. You might want to bring up your iPod controls quickly. Usually, a quick double-tap to the Home button on the bottom will bring up the 'now playing' iPod controls in the middle of the screen.

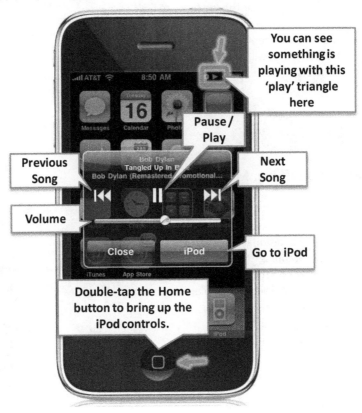

You can see something is playing with this 'play' triangle here

Pause / Play

Previous Song

Next Song

Volume

Close   iPod

Go to iPod

Double-tap the Home button to bring up the iPod controls.

If double-tapping the Home button does not bring up the controls, or you want to disable this feature, then you need to go into the Settings Icon.

Inside Settings, tap "**General**" and scroll down and tap on "**Home**." Make sure the iPod Controls near the bottom are "**ON**" or "**OFF**" to meet your needs. When you set them "**OFF**" then double-clicking the Home button will not bring up the iPod controls.

When "ON" double-clicking the Home button will bring up the iPod controls.

Repeating, Shuffling, Moving around in a Song

In the "Play" mode, you can activate additional controls by simply "tapping" the screen anywhere on the album cover. An additional slider is displayed along with the symbols for "**Repeat**," "**Shuffle**" and "**Genius**."

Moving to another Part of the Song or Video

Simply "Slide" the bar to the right and you will see the "elapsed time" of the song (which is displayed to the far right) change accordingly. If you are looking for a specific section of the song, drag the slider and then let go and listen to see if you are in the right place.

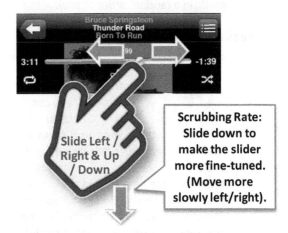

TIP: To make the slider move more slowly (fine-tune it), then drag your finger down the screen. This is also called the "Scrubbing Rate."

Repeat One Song and Repeat All Songs in Playlist or Album

To repeat the song you are listening to over just touch the "Repeat" symbol at the bottom left of the top controls twice until you see it turn blue with a "1" on it.

To repeat all songs in the playlist / song list or Album, touch the repeat icon until it turns blue (and does not have a "1") on it.

To turn off the Repeat feature, just press the icon until it turns white again.

Shuffle Icon

If you are in listening to a "Playlist" or "Album" or any other category or list of music, you might decide that you don't want to listen to the songs in their prescribed order.

Touching the "Shuffle" symbol will then "re-arrange" the music in a random order of play.

Shake to Shuffle (New in version 3.0)

 With version 3.0 of the iPhone software installed, you can now "Shake to Shuffle." In other words, to turn on the Shuffle mode, simply give your iPhone a shake.

To jump to the next song in your Shuffle, then shake it again. Every time you shake your iPhone, you will be skipped to the next randomly selected song in the list.

TIP: You can enable or disable "Shake to Shuffle" in your Settings Icon.

Tap the Settings Icon, then scroll down and touch "iPod." Then tap next to "Shake to Shuffle" to turn it "ON" or "OFF."

Genius

Apple has a new feature to iTunes called "Genius" playlists. If the "Genius" feature is activated in iTunes, it will show up here on your iPhone with the symbol shown.

Genius Playlist: Tap here to create a new playlist based on this song.

Tap

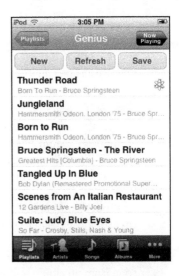

What the "Genius" feature does is create a "random" playlist by associating similar songs with the one to which you are listening. "Genius" will scour your music library and then create a new, random playlist of 25, 50 or 100 songs (you set the Genius features in iTunes on your computer.)

Use the "Genius" as a great way to "mix up" your music – playing the type of music you like but also finding some random and buried songs that may not be part of your established playlists.

TIP: Use the "Save" button at the top of the Genius screen to save your Genius playlists. After being saved, they will show with a "Genius" icon next

to them on saved playlists.

Now Playing

Sometimes, it is just too much fun to keep exploring your options for playlists, or albums that you get "buried" in a menu and find yourself just wanting to get back to the song you are listening to. Fortunately, this is always very easy to do because at the top right of any of the music screens (while in portrait mode) will be a "Now Playing" icon to touch.

Viewing other Songs on the Album

You may decide that you want to listen to another song from the particular album you are listening to as opposed to going to the next song in the playlist or genre list.

In the upper right hand corner of the screen (while in portrait mode – not in "CoverFlow" view) you will see a small button with three lines on it.

Tap that button and it will switch to a small view of the album cover and the screen will now display all the songs on that particular album.

Just touch another song in the list and that song will begin to play.

NOTE: If you start listening to another song from an album and you are in the middle of a playlist or a Genius playlist – you will not be taken back to that playlist. You will need to either go back to your playlist directory or tap "**Genius**" to make a new "**Genius**" playlist.

Tap album icon to switch back to album cover.

Blue triangle shows currently playing song.

Touch any other song to start playing it.

Adjusting Music Settings

There are several settings that you can adjust to "tweak" your music playing to your tastes. These are found in the "**Settings**" menu. Just Touch the "**Settings**" icon on your home screen.

In the middle of the Settings screen, touch the "Music" tab to bring you to the Music settings screen. There are four user adjustable settings on this screen; Sound Check, Audiobook Speed, EQ and Volume limit.

Using Sound Check ("Auto Volume Adjust")

Because many songs are recorded at different volumes, sometimes during playback a particular song might sound quite loud compared to another. Using "Sound Check" can eliminate this. If Sound Check is set to "ON" all your songs will play back at roughly the same volume.

Adjusting Audiobook Speed

Sometimes, recorded Audio Books seem to be recorded at different speeds. Some like to "slow" down the reading while other like to "speed it up." The Audiobook speed allows you to choose "Slower," "Normal" or "Faster" for the playback speed. Just select the speed you desire and then touch the "Music" tab in the upper left hand corner to return to the Music Settings Menu.

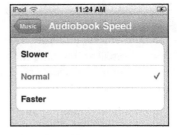

EQ (Sound Equalizer Setting)

Sound Equalization is a very personal and subjective thing. Some people like more bass in their music; some like more treble. Some like more of an exaggerated mid-range. Whatever your music tastes, there is an EQ setting for you.

Just touch the "EQ" tab and then select either the type of music you most often listen to or a specific option to boost treble or bass. Experiment, have fun and find the perfect setting that suits you.

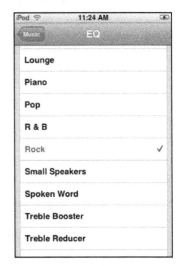

Volume Limit (Safely Listen to Music at Reasonable Volumes)

This is a great tool for parents to control the volume on their kids' iPhones. It is also a good way to stay safe and not listen too loudly through headphones so you don't damage your ears. Just move the slider to a "limit" you set and then you can "lock" that limit.

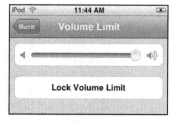

To "Lock" the volume limit – just touch the "Lock Volume Limit" button and then put in a passcode. You will be prompted to put your passcode in once more and then the volume limit will be "Locked."

Showing Music Controls when in Another Application

Let's say you were listening to music and browsing the web or checking your email at the same time. If you wanted to adjust your music, your first inclination would be to press your "Home" button and then "Touch" your Music icon.

In order for this to work, you need adjust the settings of the "Home" button as we showed you on page 39 –

Go to Settings, and then touch the "General" tab and scroll down to "Home Button" and touch the tab. Under "Double-clicking the Home Button goes to:" just select "iPod."

The easiest way to show you music controls while in another program is to actually "Double Click" the "Home" button. This will bring up just the music controls for you to adjust and you don't even have to leave the other program you are working in.

Showing Music Controls when iPhone is Locked

This even works if your iPhone is locked. Just "Double Click" the home button and the controls for adjusting the music show right up on the "locked" screen. There is no reason to "unlock" the screen and then go to the Music program to find the controls

Chapter 12:
Viewing Videos, TV Shows & More (iPod)

Your iPhone as a Video Player

The iPhone is not only a capable Music player; it is one of the best portable Video Playing systems on the market today. The Widescreen, fast processor and great Operating System make watching anything from Music Videos to TV Shows and full length motion pictures a real joy.

Loading Videos on Your iPhone

You can load Videos on your iPhone just like your music, through iTunes from your computer (page 78) or right from the iTunes icon on your iPhone (page 320).
If you purchase or rent videos and TV shows from iTunes on your computer, then you will manually or automatically sync them to your iPhone (page 84).

Watching Videos on the iPhone

Click on your iPod icon and then touch the "Video" soft key at the bottom of the screen to see the videos on your iPhone. Just touch the movie you wish to watch.

Video Categories

Your videos will be listed by category. Full-length movies will be listed first as "Movies" and "Music Videos" will be listed below.

If you have several Videos in a category (for example TV shows) you will be able to touch the tab for that TV show or Music Video category. Your iPhone will tell you how many "episodes" are contained right on the tab.

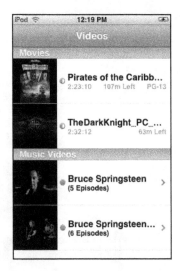

Playing a Video

Just Touch the Video you wish to watch and it will begin to play. Most Videos take advantage of the relatively large "screen real estate" of the iPhone and they play in widescreen or landscape mode. Just turn your iPhone to watch.

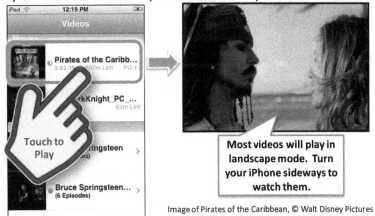

Most videos will play in landscape mode. Turn your iPhone sideways to watch them.

Image of Pirates of the Caribbean, © Walt Disney Pictures

When the Video first starts, there are no menus, no controls and nothing on the screen except for the video.

To Pause or Access Controls

Just Touch anywhere on the screen and the control bars and options will become visible. Most are very similar to those in the Music player. Just touch the "Pause" button and the video will pause.

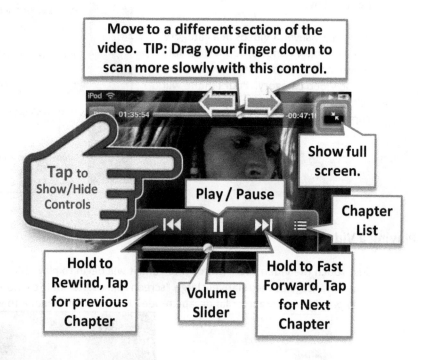

Move to a different section of the video. TIP: Drag your finger down to scan more slowly with this control.

Show full screen.

Tap to Show/Hide Controls

Play / Pause

Chapter List

Hold to Rewind, Tap for previous Chapter

Volume Slider

Hold to Fast Forward, Tap for Next Chapter

Fast Forward or Rewind the Video

On either side of the Play/Pause button are typical Fast Forward and Rewind buttons. To "Fast Forward" to the next chapter specific part of the video, just touch and hold the "FF" button (to the right of Pause/Play. When you get to the desired spot, just release the button and the Video will begin playing normally.

To Rewind to the beginning on the Video, just "Tap" the "Rewind" button. To rewind to a specific part or location, just Touch and hold like you did while you were fast forwarding the Video.

NOTE: If this is a "Full Length Movie" with several Chapters, tapping either reverse or fast forward will either move back or ahead one chapter.

Using the Time Bar

At the top of the Video screen is a "Slider" which shows you the elapsed time of the video. If you know exactly (or approximately) at which point in the Video you wish to watch, just hold and drag the slide to that location. Some people find this to be a little more exact than holding down the Fast Forward or Rewind Buttons.

TIP: Drag your finger down to move the slide more slowly. In other words, start by touching the slider control, then drag your finger down the screen -- notice that the farther down the screen your finger is, the slower the slider moves left or right. The screen may say "Scrubbing" - this just means to lower the sensitivity of how fast the slider moves.

Changing the Size of the Video (Widescreen vs. Full Screen)

Most of your Videos will play in widescreen format. However, if you have a video that was not "converted" for your iPhone or is not "optimized" for the screen resolution, you can touch the "expand" button, which is to the right of the upper Status bar.

You will notice that there are two arrows. If you are in "Full Screen" mode, the arrows are pointing in towards each other. If you are in "Widescreen" mode, the arrows are pointing outwards.

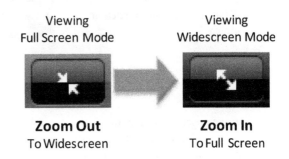

Viewing Full Screen Mode

Viewing Widescreen Mode

Zoom Out
To Widescreen

Zoom In
To Full Screen

In a Widescreen movie that is not taking up the "Full Screen" of the iPhone, touching this button will "Zoom in" a bit. Touching it again will "Zoom out."

NOTE: if you are watching a properly formatted, widescreen movie, touching this button will not do anything to alter the size of the screen. Only if you are watching a "Letterbox" or standard 4 x 3 format will the video change to fill up the screen. Be aware, that just like on your widescreen TV, when you try to "force" a non-widescreen video into widescreen mode, sometimes, you will lose part of the picture.

Using the "Chapters" Button

Most full length movies purchased from the iTunes store, and some that are "Converted" for the iPhone will give you a "Chapters" feature – very much like you were watching a DVD on your home TV.

You can scroll through the various chapters of the movie and then continue watching in that location.

Viewing the "Chapters"

Next to the Fast Forward Button you will see the "Chapters" button. This looks just like the button that you used in the Music chapter to "Flip" the album cover to show all the songs on that album.

Touch the "Chapters" button, and the video will "Flip" and you will now see all the "Chapters" of that particular movie.

You can scroll through or "Flick" through quickly to locate the scene or "Chapter" that you wish to watch. You will also notice that to the far right of each chapter is the exact time (relative to the start of the Movie) that the chapter begins.

TIP: Using Fast Forward/Reverse to Move Through Chapters

In addition to the chapter menu mentioned above, you can also quickly advance to the previous or next chapter in a movie by "Tapping" the Reverse or Fast Forward buttons. One tap moves you one chapter in either direction.

NOTE: The "Chapters" feature only works with movies that are purchased using iTunes store – movies that are "converted" and loaded on will not have "chapters."

Video Options

As in your music player, there are a few options that you can adjust for the video player. These options are accessed through the "Settings" icon from your Home Screen.

Touch the Settings Icon, then scroll down to touch "iPod" and then to the Video options.

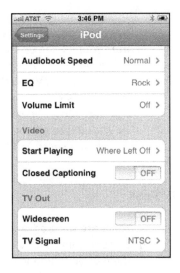

Start Playing Option

Sometimes, you will have to stop watching a particular video. This option lets you decide what to do the next time you want to watch. Your options are to either watch the video "From the Beginning" or from "Where Left Off." Just select the option that you desire and that will be the action from now on.

Closed Captioned

If your Video has Closed Captioned capabilities, when this switch is turned to "ON," Closed Captioning will be shown on your screen.

TV-Out – Widescreen

There are many third party gadgets out there that allow you to watch the video from your iPhone on some external source; either a TV or computer screen or even an array of Video Glasses that simulate watching on a very large screen monitor. Most of these require that your TV Widescreen setting be set to "**On**." By default, it is set to "**off**."

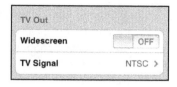

TV Signal

There are some advanced ways of taking content from your TV or DVR and playing them on your iPhone with the right cable. You also need to have the right TV signal setting. This is only to be changed if you use your iPhone in another country. If you live in the U.S., your TV works with the NTSC standard. European countries mostly use PAL. If you are not sure which you use, contact your Cable or Satellite company.

Deleting Videos

To Delete a Video (to save space on your iPhone) just open up your video list as you did at the start of this chapter.

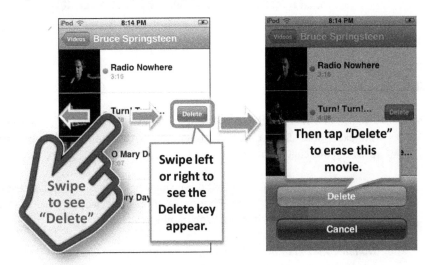

Swipe left or right with your finger (don't tap to open) and you will see a small, red "Delete" tab appear. Just touch the "Delete" tab.

The next window asks you to confirm the Delete. Touch the red "Delete" bar and the video will be deleted from your system.

NOTE: This only deletes the video from your iPhone – a copy will still remain in your video library in iTunes if you want to once again load it back onto your iPhone.

Chapter 13:
Connecting to a Wi-Fi Network

The Benefits of Wi-Fi

We live in a Wi-Fi world. Wireless Internet access has become the rule, not the exception. Sometimes, you might find yourself out of the "Coverage" area of your cellular provider - in a basement, in a building, etc.

The beauty of the iPhone is that it has built in Wireless Internet access. You just have to "Connect" your iPhone to a wireless network and you can be sending email and surfing the Web in minutes.

Do I need Wi-Fi to download some Apps and larger files?
Yes. Some larger Applications (usually over about 8 megabytes) will require you to connect your iPhone via Wi-Fi to the web in order to install the App or large file you purchased.

Searching for a Network

The first thing to do is to go to your "**Settings**" icon on your Home Screen. Tap the **"Wi-Fi"** tab at the top to see the screen shown. Make sure that the Wi-Fi button is set to **"ON"** by tapping it if it is **"OFF."**
Once Wi-Fi is **"ON,"** the iPhone will automatically begin to start looking for Wireless networks.

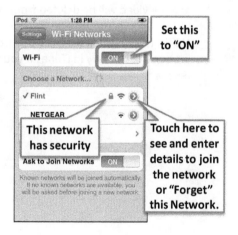

The list of available Networks will be shown under where it says: "Choose a Network..." You can see in this screen shot that I have two networks from which to choose.

Connecting to a Network

In order to connect to any Network listed, just touch it. If the network is unsecure (does not require a password), you will be connected automatically.

Secure Networks - Entering a Password

Some Networks require a password to "log-in." This is set when the network administrator originally created the wireless network. Make sure you have the exact password and know if it is "case sensitive."

If the network does require a password, you will be taken to the password entry screen. Type the password exactly as given to you and select "Join" at the bottom right of the screen.

TIP: Some conventions, offices, restaurants or other locations do require a password. If so, just ask someone in charge.

Once you touch "Join" you will go back to the Network screen and you will see a checkmark showing that you are connected to the network.

Verifying Your Wi-Fi Connection

Touch the "Settings" button in the top left corner of the Wi-Fi Networks screen. You will be taken back to the "Settings" screen. You should now see the name of your Wi-Fi network next to where it says "Wi-Fi."

Advanced Wi-Fi Options ("Hidden" or "Undiscoverable" Networks)

Why can I not see the Wi-Fi Network I want to join?
Sometimes, for security reasons, people to not make their networks "discoverable" and you will have to manually enter the name and security options to connect.

Under your list of available networks, you will see that is says "Other..." Touch the "Other" tab, and you can manually enter in the name of a Network you would like to join.

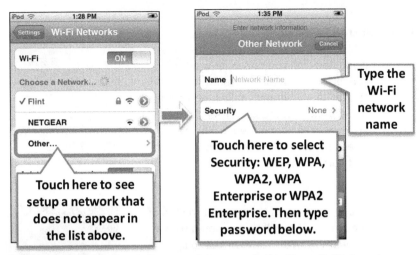

Type in the Wi-Fi Network Name and then touch the "Security" tab and choose which type of security is being used on that network. If you are unsure, you will need to acquire this information from the Network Administrator.

Then, just input the proper password and this new network will be saved to your network list for future access.

Ask to Join Networks

By default, this switch is set to "ON" and you will join "known" or "visible" Wi-Fi networks automatically. If Networks are available which are not known to you, you will be asked before being connected to the network.

If the switch is set to "OFF," you will only be automatically connected to "Known" networks and you will have to follow the procedure above for "Manually" joining unknown networks.

Why might someone do this? This could be a good security measure if you don't want your kids to be automatically able to join a wireless network on the iPhone.

Forget (or Erase) a Network

If you find that you no longer want to connect to a network on your list you can "forget" it – essentially take it off your list of networks. Just touch the small blue arrow next to your network. The next screen shows all the network details of that particular connection.

Touch "Forget this Network" at the top of the screen. You will be prompted with a red warning. You can then just touch "Forget Network" and the network will no longer show up on your list

Chapter 14:
Surfing the Web (Safari)

Web Browsing on the iPhone

You can browse the web to your heart's content via Wi-Fi or with your iPhone's cellular connection. The iPhone has what many feel is the most capable mobile browsing experience available today. Web pages look like Web Pages on your computer. With the iPhone's ability to "Zoom" in, you don't even have to worry about the small screen size inhibiting your web browsing experience.

How do you know when you can browse the web on your iPhone?

Check out our Network Connectivity overview on page 19 and our Network Speed Overview on page 21.

Launching the Web Browser

By default, the Safari (Web Browser) icon is loaded in your bottom dock. If you have not moved it, it should be at the bottom right of your iPhone – in the dock. If you did move your Safari icon, you will need to locate it on your home screen.

Touch the Safari icon and you will be taken to the "Home Page" of your browser. Most likely, this will be the Apple iPhone Home page – but you can change that – we will show you how in just a few pages.

Layout of Screen

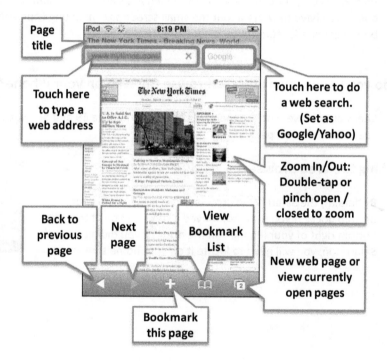

As you look at your screen, you should notice that the "Address Bar" is in the upper left hand side of the screen. This displays the current web address. Next to that is the "Search" window. By default, this is set to "Google" search, but you can always change that later.

At the bottom of the screen are 5 icons; **"Back," "Forward," "Add Bookmark," "Bookmarks"** and **"Pages view."**

Typing a Web Address (URL - Example: www.google.com)

The first thing you'll want to learn how to do is to get to your favorite web pages. You type in the web address (URL) just like on your computer's web browser. To start typing, tap the address bar at the top of the browser. You will then see the keyboard appear and the window for the browser expand. Start typing and press the "GO" key to go to that page.

TIP: Remember to use the ".com" key at the bottom to save some time.

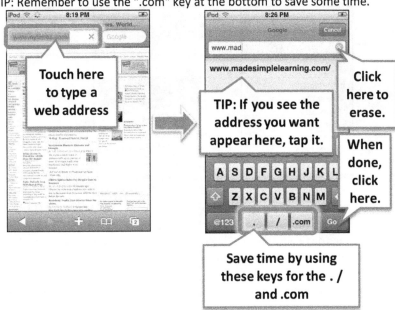

TIP: Press and hold the .com key to see all the options like: .org, .edu, .net, .de, etc.

Booking Your Travel Reservations

There are several travel web sites that you can use to book your airline, hotel and rental car on your iPhone. Orbitz (www.orbitz.com) and Travelocity (www.travelocity.com) are just a couple of examples. Travelocity recently launched an iPhone-friendly travel site. You will probably find more web sites with iPhone-friendly versions by the time you read this book.

The other option is to use an "App" specifically designed for travel reservations. To locate the App, start up the App Store icon and perform a search to find Apps that specialize in "travel reservations." Learn more in our chapter on the App Store starting on page 338.

Moving to Backwards or Forwards through Open Web Pages

Now that you know how to enter web addresses, you will probably be jumping to various web sites. The "Forward" and "Back" arrows make it very easy to advance to pages just visited in either direction.

Let's say you were on the New York Times Web site looking at the news and then you jumped to ESPN to check sports scores. To go "Back" to the NY Times page, just hit the "**Back**" arrow. To Go "Forwards" to the ESPN site again, just touch the "**Forward**" arrow.

Adding Bookmarks, Add Icon to Home Screen, Mail Page Links

Just like on your home computer, you can set "Bookmarks" on your iPhone. To add a new Bookmark, simply touch the "Plus" sign in the bottom of the web screen.

After touching the **"+"** sign you will see three options. Choose **"Add Bookmark"** to add a new bookmark. You could also **"Add to Home Screen"** (puts a handy icon on your home screen), or **"Mail Link to this Page"** which will allow you to email the link to the current page to anyone.

Touch here to Add a Bookmark, Add to Home Screen (icon) or Email a link to this page

After you touch **"Add Bookmark"** you may edit the name of the bookmark (the web address is shown underneath the editing window. You can also choose in which folder you would like the bookmark to appear. By default, the bookmark will go in your "Bookmark" folder, but you can also place it in any of the folders that are available to you (News, Popular or Bookmarks Menu.)
Press "**Save**" to save your changes.

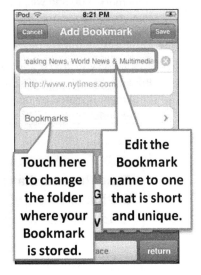

Touch here to change the folder where your Bookmark is stored.

Edit the Bookmark name to one that is short and unique.

Using your Bookmarks

Once Bookmarks are set, as shown above, simply touch the "**Bookmark**" icon from any web page to see your Bookmarks.

When you first touch the **"Bookmarks"** icon, you can see tabs for your **"History,"** **"Bookmarks Bar"** and **"Bookmarks Menu."** Under that will be pre-installed Bookmarks for your iPhone.

Bookmarks you add will, by default, go into your "Bookmarks Bar" unless you specify another spot.

TIP: When you are creating your Bookmarks, adjust the folder where the bookmark is stored by tapping the Folder name under the name of the Bookmark.

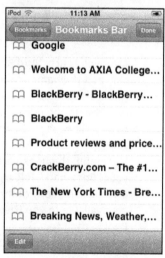

Touch here to change the folder where your Bookmark is stored.

Adding Folders, Editing and Deleting Bookmarks

It is very easy to accumulate quite a collection of bookmarks since it is so easy to set them up. You may find that you no longer need a particular bookmark in your list or want to organize your Bookmarks by adding new Folders.

In order to manage your bookmarks, tap the "Edit" button at the bottom left corner of your "Bookmarks" menu.

You will notice that a red (-) minus sign appears to the left and each bookmark turns into a tab that can be touched.

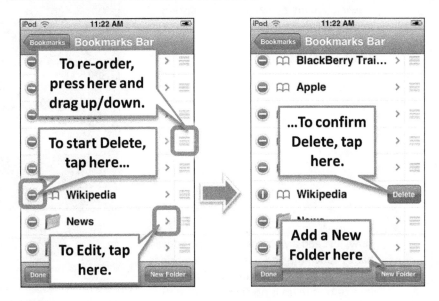

To Delete the bookmark, just touch the red "Minus Sign" and you will see the "**Delete**" button pop up. Touch "**Delete**," confirm the Delete and the bookmark will no longer be in your menu.

RE-ORDER BOOKMARKS:
Just touch and drag the icon in the left edge of each bookmark to re-order it.

NEW BOOKMARK FOLDERS:
To add a new folder, touch the "**New Folder**" button in the lower right corner. Type the name of the Folder, select the location (folder) in which to place your new folder, and click "**Done**"

Using the New Pages Button

On our home computers, many of us have come to rely on "tabbed" browsing which allows us to have more than one web page open at a time so we can quickly move from one to the other. The iPhone has a similar feature available to you by touching the "New Page" icon at the very bottom right corner of the web screen.

The first time you touch this button, you notice that the web page you are currently viewing becomes small and moved to the middle of the screen.

Touch the "**New Page**" button in the lower left corner and you will see a new, small page in the center of the screen.

Now, just add a web address in the address bar by touch the address bar (which brings up the keyboard.) Type in your web address (notice that there is no "space Bar" in this keyboard – Just touch the "." For the "dot" or the ".com" button to fill out the web site if it has "com" as the extension at the end of the name.

Now when you touch the **"New Page"** icon, you can just swipe through your open pages and choose which web site you wish to view. Just touch the page you wish to view and it will load into the screen.

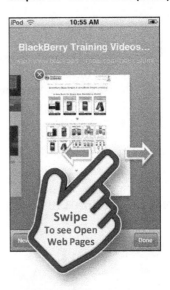

Once the page loads, and you click **"Done"** in the lower right corner, you should see the little number in the lower right hand screen change from 1 to 2 – indicating that there are two "tabs" or "pages" open.

Zooming in and Out in Web Pages

Zooming in and out of web pages is very easy on the iPhone. There are two primary ways of zooming; "Double Tapping" and "Pinching."

Double Tapping

If you tap twice (double tap) on a column of a web page, the page will zoom in on that particular column. This makes it convenient to zoom in on exactly the right place on the web page. This is helpful on pages that are not specifically formatted for a mobile screen.

To "Zoom Out" just "Double Tap" once more. See graphically how this looks on page 28.

Pinching Open or Pinching Closed

"Pinching" is a technique you can use in Web Pages and in Pictures to "Zoom" in on a particular section of the page. It takes a little bit of practice, but will soon become second nature.

See graphically how this looks on page 29.

Use your thumb and forefinger and place them close together at the section of the web page you wish to zoom into. Slowly "Pinch out" – separating your fingers. You will see the web page then zoom in. It takes a couple of seconds for the web page to "focus," but it will zoom in and be very clear after a short while.

To "Zoom Out" to where you were before, just start with your fingers apart and move them slowly together – the page will zoom out to its original size.

New in Version 3.0: Copying and Pasting from a Web Page

 With 3.0 software you can copy and paste text from a web page. We show you how on page 57

Activating Links from Web Pages

Often times, when surfing the Web, you will come across a "link" that will take you to another web site. Because the Safari Web Browser is a full functioning browser, you can just touch the link and you will jump to a new page.

If you want to return to the previous page, just press the "Back" arrow as shown earlier.

Installing Software from a Web Link

Sometimes, the web link you touch will ask you to download software. This is most common if there is an iPhone or iPhone "specific" site that has been established for that page.

iPhone/iPhone Specific Sites

iPhone and iPhone specific sites are essentially "Free Apps" that are downloaded from the App store see page 340.

Many of these sites can actually be installed by visiting the "regular" web site and then touching the link to download and install the iPhone/iPhone specific program.

In this example, we typed in
www.weather.com on our Browser.

We were notified in the middle of the
web page that there was a specific
iPhone/iPhone interface to download.

Touch that link to be brought to the
download page.

When I touch the link, I am taken right to
the App Store and the download link for
this software. I touch the "**FREE**" button,
which changes to a "**DOWNLOAD**" button.
Touch "**DOWNLOAD**" to start the
download.

Once the download is finished, the button
changes to "**INSTALL**." Touch the
"**INSTALL**" button to get the program
being installed on your Home screen.

Finally, you will see the fully installed new "App" or Icon on your Home Screen.

From now on, the Weather Channel (www.weather.com) site is just a touch away using the new icon on my Home Screen.

Many web sites, including The New York Times and AP News, among many others, have built iPhone/iPod Touch specific sites that load more quickly and take advantage of the iPhone interface.

Adjusting Web Browsing Settings

Like other "Settings" we have adjusted so far, the settings for the Safari Browser are found in the "Settings" Icon.

Just Touch the "Settings" icon and scroll down to "Safari" and touch.

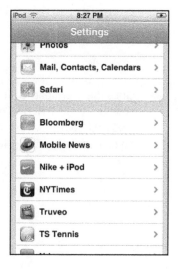

Changing the Search Engine (Google, Yahoo, More)

By default, the Search Engine for the Safari Browser is "**Google**." To change this to "**Yahoo**," touch the "**Search Engine**" tab and then choose "**Yahoo**" instead of Google.

Adjusting Browser Security Options

Under the "Security" heading, you should see that "**JavaScript**," **Plug-ins**" and "**Block Pop-ups**" should all, by default, be set to "**ON**." You can adjust any of these by just sliding the switch to "**OFF**."

Under these switches is the "**Accept Cookies**" tab. This can be adjusted to accept "Cookies" either: "**Always**," "**Never**" or "**From Visited**."

Speed Up Your Browser: Clear History & Clear Cookies

On the bottom of the Safari settings screen, you will see the "**Clear History**" and "**Clear Cookies**" buttons.

If you notice your web browsing getting a bit sluggish, that might be a good time to go and clear out both the "**History**" and "**Cookies.**"

TIP: It is also a good privacy measure to prevent others from seeing where you have been browser.

Occasionally, it is a good idea to clear out your history and your cookies.

iPhone 3.0 Feature: Auto Fill Name, Password, Email, Address & More

New in iPhone 3.0 OS is the ability to automatically fill out web forms that call for your name, password, email address, etc. This is a common feature on PC or Mac based browsers, but a first for the iPhone.

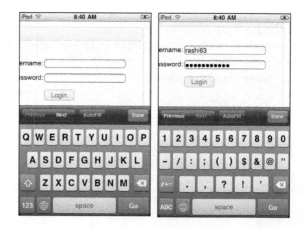

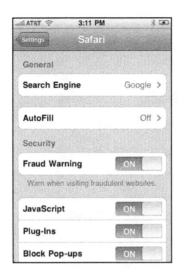 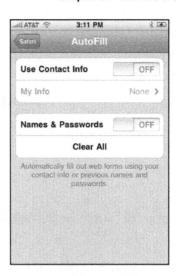

Using Browsing History To Save Time and Find Sites

The advantage to keeping your frequently visited sites in the history is that you can load them from the"History" tab when you go into the Browser menu. Also, sometimes you know that you want to go back to a certain site, but you can't remember the name – checking the history will show you the exact site you wish to visit.

Chapter 15:
Email on your iPhone

Your iPhone for "Anywhere, Anytime" Access to Email

Mobile email is certainly all the rage today. Depending on your wireless carrier (phone company) you will typically have unlimited email Included in your iPhone data plan. With the iPhone, mobile email is available via your wireless (cellular) signal and your Wi-Fi connection. (For help with Wi-Fi, see page 197.)

How do you know when you can send or receive email on your iPhone?

After you setup email on your iPhone, you still need to have the right network connectivity to send and receive email. Check out our Network Connectivity overview on page 19 and our Network Speed Overview on page 21 to learn more.

Setting up Email on the iPhone

On page 97, we showed you how to sync the setup information (login, username, password, etc.) of your email accounts using iTunes. If this was done properly, the your email accounts may already be in your Touch and "Active."

The easiest way to check and see if your email accounts are already set up is to go through the "**Settings**" Icon.

Touch the "**Settings**" icon and scroll down to "**Mail, Contacts and Calendars**" and touch the tab.
Under "**Accounts**", you should see your email accounts listed.

Adding a New Account from "Settings"

To add a new email account from the "**Settings**" menu, just touch "**Add Account**" below your email accounts. If you have no accounts set up, you will only see the "**Add Account**" option.

TIP: To Edit any Email account, just touch that account.

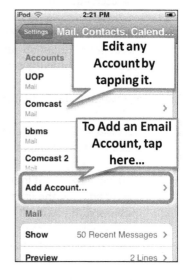

Choose which type of email account to add from the next screen. If you are a "Microsoft Exchange User" (most likely, this is only for enterprise users) you would touch "Microsoft Exchange."

If you use Apple's "Mobile me" service to wirelessly sync your information, you would touch the "Mobile me" icon. If you don't have a Gmail, Yahoo Mail or AOL account – just touch "Other" to set up a standard POP or IMAP email account.

Input your Name, as you would like others to see it when they receive mail from you. Then, add your Email address, Password and a short description of the account.

Just touch "Save" and you will be taken to the next screen – either you account will be set up automatically or you will have to specify information about your particular account.

Specifying Incoming and Outgoing Servers

Just like setting up an email account on your computer, sometimes you will need to manually input the settings of your particular account.

You will have to put in the incoming mail server address, the user name and the password. If you don't know these settings, contact your ISP (Internet Service Provider) and they will be able to provide them for you. Usually, your incoming mail server is something like mail.nameofyourisp.com.

Once your input the information for your incoming server, you will now need to specify the information for your outgoing server.

In the outgoing server information, you put in the outgoing server address – usually either **smtp.nameofyourisp.com** or **mail.nameofyourisp.com**. You can try to leave the name and password blank – if it doesn't work, you can go back and change it.

You may be asked if you want to use SSL (secure socket layer) – a type of outgoing mail security that may be required by your ISP. If you don't know whether you need it or not, just check the mail settings with your ISP.

Verifying that your Account is Set Up

Once all the information is put in, the iPhone will attempt to configure your email account. You may get an error message – in which case you need to review the information you input.

If you are taken to the screen that shows all your email accounts, look for the new account name. If you see it, your account was set up correctly.

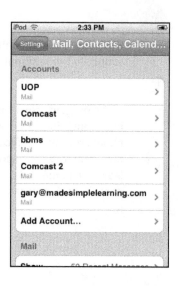

Getting Started With Mail

To launch the Email program, just touch the "Mail" icon on your home screen. The first screen you will see is the list of your accounts. The iPhone will begin to check for new mail and then display the number of new messages for each account.

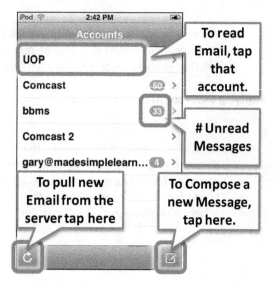

Composing a New Email Message

When you start the "Mail" program, your first screen should be your "Accounts" screen. At the bottom right hand corner of the screen, you will see the "Compose" icon. Just touch the "Compose" icon to get started creating a new message.

Addressing Your Message - Choose the Recipients

Then, you need to address your message, you have several options depending on whether or not the person is in your Contact List

Option 1: Type an email address - notice the "@" and "." keys on the bottom to help you typing.

Option 2: Type a few letters of someone's first name; hit the "space" key, and a few letters of their last name. The person's name should appear on the list, tap to select their name.

Option 3: Hit the "+" sign to view your entire Contact List and search/select a name from it.

DELETING A RECIPIENT:

If you need to delete a name from the recipient list (To:, Cc: or Bcc:), tap the name and hit the backspace key.

TIP: If you want to delete the last recipient you typed (and the cursor is sitting next to that name), just hit the delete key once to select the name and again to delete it.

Choose which Email Account to Send From

If you have more than one Email account set up, the iPhone will use whichever account you designated as the "Default" account. If you want to specify an account to have as the sending account for this email, just touch the "From" line and all your Email Accounts will be displayed at the bottom. Just choose the "sending" account from the list.

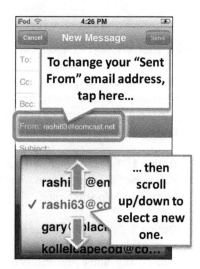

Type in a Subject

Touch the "**Subject**" line and enter in text for the subject of the email and press the Enter key or tap in the "Body" area of the email.

Type Your Message

Now that the cursor is in your "Body" section (under the subject line), you can start typing your email message.

EMAIL SIGNATURES: If you have set up an Email Signature for the account you are using, it will be displayed at the bottom of the body of the email message. See page 234 to learn how to change your email signature.

iPhone 3.0 Feature: Landscape Keyboard

One of the challenging things about writing emails on the iPhone has been the "Portrait" keyboard with its small keys. iPhone users will be very happy to know that in version 3.0, you can now tilt your iPhone into the "Horizontal" position and use a "Landscape" keyboard for composing Email – giving you much larger keys to work with.

Send your Email

Once you have typed your message and proof read the text, just touch the blue "Send" button in the top right hand corner. Your Email will send and you should hear the "sent" sound that is played on the iPhone, confirming that your mail was sent.

Checking Sent Messages

To Confirm that the Email was sent, just go to the Account folder of the account you just used to send the last message. You should see an "Inbox," a "Sent" folder and a "Trash" folder.

Go into the Sent folder and you should see the latest email that was just "Sent."

NOTE: You will only see the "Sent" and "Trash" folders if you have actually sent or deleted email from that account on the iPhone. If your Email account is an IMAP account, you will see many folders other than those listed above.

Reading and Replying to Mail

Just touch one of the mail tabs and you will see your email for that particular email account. The first screen shows your inbox, outbox and trash for that particular account.

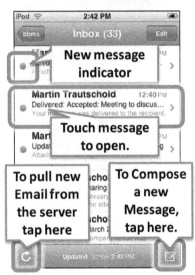

To read your messages, just touch your "Inbox." New, unread messages are shown with a small blue dot to the left of the message – just like in the Mail program on Mac Computers.

You can scroll through your messages by moving your finger and flicking through the messages. When you want to read a message, just touch that message.

Scroll through your email just like you scroll through a web page.

Zooming in

Just like browsing the web, you can "Zoom in" to see your email in larger text. You can "Double Tap" (see page 28) just as you did with the web and you can also "Pinch" to zoom in – see page 29.

Reply, Forward or Delete Message

At the bottom of your email-reading pane is a tool bar.

From this you can move the message to a different Mailbox/folder, Delete it or Reply/Reply All/Forward.

Touch the small arrow to see the option buttons appear of "**Reply**," "**Reply All**" and "**Forward**."
NOTE: "**Reply All**" is only an option if there was more than just one recipient to an email.

Replying to an Email

Most likely the "**Reply**" command is the one you will use most often. Just touch the "**Reply**" button.

You will now see that the original "Sender" is now listed as the "Recipient" in the "To:" line of the email.

The subject will automatically state: "Re: *(Original subject line)*."

Type your response using the keyboard. When you are done, just touch the blue "**Send**" button at the top right hand corner of the screen.

Version 3.0 Feature: Type Faster with 2 Thumbs in Landscape (Horizontal) Mode

With version 3.0 software installed on your iPhone, you can simply turn the iPhone sideways to type with a larger keyboard. (Learn how to upgrade to 3.0 software on page 364.) This is great for people like the authors who have larger fingers. TIP: It is much easier to type with your thumbs when the keyboard is larger - a la "BlackBerry" thumb typing. Once you get the hang of "thumb-typing," you will find that It is much faster than typing with one finger on the keyboard. See page 47 for many more typing tips.

Using "Reply All"

Using "**Reply All**" is just like using the "**Reply**" function, except all of the original recipients of the email and the original sender are placed in the address lines. The original sender will be in the "To:" line and the other recipients of the original email will be listed on the "Cc:" line.

Using the "Forward" Button

Sometimes, you get an email that you want to send on to someone else. The "**Forward**" command will let you do that.

IMPORTANT - FORWARD ATTACHMENTS:
If you want to send someone any attachments from an email you receive, you must choose "Forward." ("Reply" and "Reply All" will not include the original email attachments in your outgoing message.)

When you do touch the "Forward" button. You may be prompted to either "**Include**" or "**Don't Include**" attachments (if there were any) from the original message.

Then, you need to address the message using the same techniques as we showed you above. Type a few letters to select a person from your address book, type an email address or touch the blue "+" sign to find someone from your contact list.

Type a short note if desired, or just press the blue "**Send**" button to send on the forwarded message.

Deleting Email Messages

As you get more and more comfortable with your iPhone as an Email device, you will find yourself using the "Mail" program more and more. It will become necessary to occasionally do some "Email Housecleaning" and delete Email messages you no longer need on your device.

Deleting from the Inbox

Deleting messages is very easy on the iPhone. Just go into one of your mail accounts and start to view your list of messages. These will most likely be found in your "Inbox" for that particular account.

In the upper right hand corner of the screen, you will see the "**Edit**" button. Just touch the edit button and the view of the screen changes. You should see open circles next to each message with two buttons on the bottom of screen; a "Red" one that says Delete and a "Blue" one that says "Move."

Just touch the open circles next to the messages you wish to "Delete." This will put a red check mark in the circle. Touch as many of these circles as you want.

Once your emails are selected for deletion, just touch the red "Delete" button and the message will be deleted. You do not get another prompt before the delete, so be sure that you do want to delete the message. While the message will be deleted on your device, a copy will still remain on the server.

Deleting from the Message Screen

Another way to delete messages can be found in the "Message Viewing" screen. Just open any message to read. Notice the icons at the bottom of the Screen.

In the middle, you will see an icon of a trash can. Just touch that icon and the email you are reading will get "Sucked down" right into the trash can and deleted.

Moving Email Messages

Email Messages can be moved out of your inbox for storage or for reading at another time. Moving messages is as easy as deleting them and is handled in a similar fashion.

Moving from the Inbox

Just as you did with "Deleting" a message, navigate to your inbox of the particular account from which you desire to "Move" a message.

Once again, Touch the "Edit" key in the upper right hand corner. Select the messages to "Move" by placing a red check mark in the circles next to the messages you want to move.

This time, touch the blue "Move" button which should show a small number indicating how many messages you have checked to move.

You may not have many folders in which to move your messages, but you will always have a "**Trash**" option in addition to the "Inbox."

Select the "**Trash**" option or any other folder that may be available to you, and the messages will be moved to that location.

Moving from a Message itself

Open a message to read and notice the five icons at the bottom of the screen. Choose the icon that is second from the left – the "**Move**" icon that looks like a small folder.

Just as before, choose the new folder and the message will be moved out of the inbox.

Email Search- New 3.0 Feature

The iPhone 3.0 OS adds some search functionality to your emails as well. Now, you can Search your inbox by the "From," "To," "Subject" or "All" fields. This helps you filter your inbox to see exactly what you are searching for.

Activating Email Search

Get to the "Inbox" of the account you wish to search. If you scroll up to the top, you will now see the familiar "Search Bar" at the top of your inbox. Just touch the search bar and a new menu of "soft keys" shows under the search bar.

Type in the text you wish to search and then tough the appropriate soft key. So, if I wanted to search my inbox for an email I received from Martin, I would type in Martin's name in the search box and then touch "**From.**" My inbox would be filtered to show only the email that was from Martin.

NOTE: If you have multiple email accounts, you will not be able to search all of your inboxes at the same time – you can only search one inbox at a time. For a more global search, just use the "Spotlight Search" highlighted above.

Setting your Email Options

There are many user-configurable options that you can adjust for your Email accounts.

Touch the "**Settings**" icon from your home screen. Now, scroll down to touch "**Mail, Contacts, Calendars**."

Adjusting the Mail Settings

Under the account list are the Mail Settings. You will see the word "**Mail**" and then adjustable settings underneath. In most cases, the "**Default**" settings should work well for you.

You can adjust how many Email messages are shown, the default is 50 Recent Messages and this can be adjusted to show up to 200 messages by touching the tab and changing the setting.

You may Preview up to 5 lines of your messages by touching the "**Preview**" tab and adjusting the settings.

You may adjust the Minimum Font size to any one of 5 size options by touching this tab and choosing the setting.

There are three "switches" for "**Show To/Cc Label**," "**Ask Before Deleting**" and "**Always Bcc Myself**." These are all turned "**OFF**" by default, but can be adjusted by just sliding them to the "**ON**" position.

Changing your Email Signature

By default, Emails you send will say "Sent from my iPhone" unless you change the "Signature line" of the email.

Just Touch the "**Signature**" tab and type in the new Email Signature you want at the bottom of emails sent from the iPhone.

When you are done with the new Signature, just Tap the "**Mail**" button in the upper left hand corner and you will be returned to the Mail settings menu.

Changing your Default Mail Account (Sent From)

If you have multiple Email Accounts set up on your iPhone, you should set one of them – usually, the one you use most, as your Default account. When you simply select "Compose" from the Email screen, the default account is always chosen.

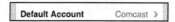

Just Touch the "Default Account" tab and you will see a list of all your Email accounts. Simply Touch the one you wish to use as your "Default Account. When you are done, touch the "**Mail**" tab again in the upper left hand corner, and you will return to the Mail Settings menu.

Troubleshooting Email Problems

Usually, if you follow all the steps above, your email will perform seamlessly and you will be retrieving, forwarding and composing new emails before you know it. Sometimes, whether it is a server issue or an ISP requirement, email may not be as flawless as we hope.

More often than not, there is a simple setting that needs to be adjusted or a password re-entered.

Checking your Account Settings

Go to the "**Settings**" icon and then to "**Mail, Contacts, Calendars.**" If you received an error message from a particular account, touch the tab for that account.

Check that the "**Host Name**," "**User Name**" and "**Password** "are correct. If you received an error message while trying to "Send" an email, the issue will be most likely in your SMTP settings – the settings that the email program uses to access your mail server to send mail.

Touch the SMTP tab for the account that is giving you trouble. Touch on the "**Primary Server**" tab and make sure that it is set to "**On.**" Underneath, you will see other SMTP servers that are used for your other email accounts. One option is to use one of the other SMTP servers that you know is working – just touch the tab for that server and turn the switch to "**On.**"

Using SSL

Some SMTP servers require the use of "Secure Socket Layer" security. If you are having trouble sending email and the "**Use SSL**" switch is set to "**OFF**" try setting it to "**ON**" and see if that helps.

Changing the method of Authentication

Under the SSL switch is an "Authentication" tab – usually, "Password" is the correct setting. We don't recommend that you change this setting unless you have specific directions from your ISP to make a change.

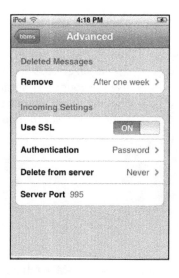

Changing the Server Port

Most often, when you configure your Email account, the server port is set for you. Sometimes, there are "tweaks" that need to be made that are specific to your ISP.

If you have been given specific settings from your ISP, you can change the server port to try to alleviate and errors you might be receiving.

To change the server port, go back to the specific SMTP settings for your account. Touch the tab for the Primary Server, as you did in the previous step.

Scroll down to "Server Port" and touch the screen on the number indicated. A keyboard will pop up and you can input a new number (the one given you by your ISP.) Most often, the number shows will be 995, 993, 587 or 110 – but if you have a different number, just input it. When you are done, touch the SMTP tab in the upper left hand corner to return to the previous screen.

Advanced Email Options

There are a few "Advanced" Email features available to experienced users. To find the Advanced features, just touch the tab for any of your email accounts. Scroll down to "**Advanced**" and touch the screen on that tab.

Remove Email Messages from iPhone After Deletion

You can select how frequently you want Email removed completely from your iPhone once it is deleted. Touch the "Remove" tab and select the option that is best for you – the default setting is "**After one week.**"

USE SSL/Authentication

These features were discussed above, but this is another location to access those features for this particular account.

Delete from Server

You can configure your iPhone to handle the deleting of messages from your Email server. Usually, this setting is left at '**Never**" and this function is handled on your main computer. If you use your iPhone ad your main Email device, you might want to handle that feature from here.

Touch the "**Delete from Server**" tab and you can select the feature that best suits your needs; "**Never**," "**Seven Days**" or "**When removed from Inbox**." The default setting is "**Never**." If you want to choose "**Seven Days**" that should give you enough time to check email on your computer as well as your iPhone and then decide what to keep and what to get rid of.

Change Incoming Server Port

As you did with the "Outgoing Server Port" above, you can also change the incoming server port if you are having trouble "receiving" email. It is very rare that your troubles will be related to "receiving" mail – so it is rare that you would need to change this number. If your ISP gives you a different number, just touch the numbers and input a new port. Incoming Server Ports are usually 995, 993, 110 or it could be another number your ISP gives you.

Automatically Retrieve Email

You can set your iPhone to "manually" retrieve email (meaning that you tell it when to get the mail, or you can set it to have "New Data" "Pushed" to the device at set intervals.

Having automatic retrieval is very handy if you just want to turn on your iPhone and see that you have messages – otherwise, you need to remember to check.

Setting up "Push" options

From your Home screen, touch the "**Settings**" icon and then touch the "**Mail, Contacts and Calendars tab.

Under your email accounts you will see a tab that says "**Fetch New Data**." Touch the "**Fetch New Data**" tab.

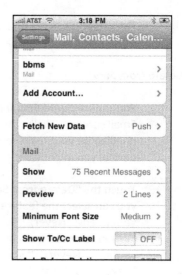

The first thing to do, if you want your email or other data "Pushed" to your iPhone is to set the **"Push"** switch to **"On."**

Next, under where it says "Fetch," you can choose whether to have the iPhone "Fetch" your data every 15, 30 or 60 minutes or to fetch data manually. Just touch the option that will work best for you.

REMEMBER: That if you set this for 15 or 30 minutes you will experience some battery drain as the iPhone will be "Going online" at those intervals to get your data.

Advanced "Push" options

Touch the **"Advanced"** tab and you will see a new screen showing you all your accounts that can be "Fetched." You can decide to "Fetch" only one or some (if you have multiple email accounts.)

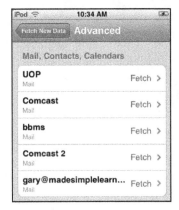

This is helpful if you have a "Primary" account or if you are expecting an important email on one of your accounts and you don't want to keep "manually" checking to see if it comes in.

Setting Sounds for Receiving and Sending Mail

If you would like to be alerted to new Email via a sound on your iPhone or if you want a "confirmation" sound once email is sent, this is as simple as setting a switch.

Just Start your "**Settings**" App and then scroll down to "**General**" and touch the tab. Next, scroll to "**Sounds**" and touch the tab. You will see two switches for "**New Mail**" and "**Sent Mail**." Just move the switches to "**ON**" if you would like sound for these events.

Email Troubleshooting

Sometimes, your Email doesn't behave as you would like – here are a few steps to take if you have trouble.

Email isn't Being Sent

Sometimes, you need to adjust the outgoing "Port" for Email to be sent properly. As you did above, go into "**Settings**" and touch the tab for you Email account and then touch "**Advanced**." Try a different port setting for the "Outgoing Server Port." Try 587 or 995 or 110. If those don't work, contact your ISP to get a different port number.

Can't open Email Attachments

The "Mail" app on the iPhone can handle many types of attachments that may come through via email – but not all. The attachments supported on the iPhone are:

> .doc and .docx (Word Documents)
> .htm and .html (web page)
> .key (Keynote Presentation)
> .numbers (Apple Numbers Spreadsheet)
> .pages (Apples Pages document)
> . pdf (adobe Reader file)
> . ppt and .pptx (PowerPoint Presentations)
> .txt (text files)
> .vcf (contact information)
> .xls and .xlsx (Excel Spreadsheets)

Make sure your attachment is not some other, non-supported format type.

Chapter 16:
Working with Contacts

Importing Contacts from Other Programs

On page 92 we showed you how to import and synchronize your contacts from your computer using iTunes. Once your contacts are set up for being Synced with your iPhone, they will update each time you connect your iPhone to your PC or Mac.

Just make sure you have you iTunes set to Synchronize with whatever your contact management program may be and you should be continually "In Sync" with your PC or Mac.

You can also wirelessly synchronize or share contacts with your iPhone depending on which software or services you use. Learn more on page 92.

TIP: You can also add new Contact entries from Email Messages you receive. Learn how on page 250.

Adding a New Contact

You always have the option of adding your contacts right on your iPhone. You might find yourself away from your computer, but carrying your iPhone and you need to add someone to your "Contacts" – this is very easy to do.

Start the Contacts Icon

From your Home Screen, just Touch the "**Contacts**" icon and you will see your Contact list. Just touch the blue "+" sign in the upper right hand corner to add a new contact.

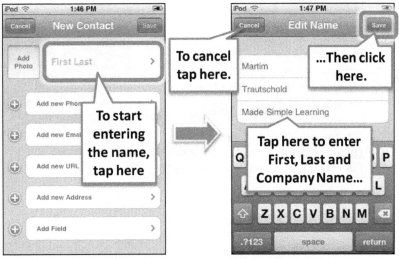

Touch the "**First Last**" button and input the new contact's first and last name. You may also add a "Company" as well.

Under the "**First Last**" button are five more buttons. Each is activated by either; touching the green "+" sign to the left of the button or just touching the button itself.

Adding a New Phone Number

Touch the "**Add new Phone**" button and use the number pad to input the phone number.

TIP: Don't worry about parentheses, dashes or dots, the iPhone will put the number into the correct format – just type the digits of the area code and number.

TIP: You can also add a new Contact Entry from your "Recents" icon inside the Phone icon. Learn how on page 108.

Adding "Pauses" (Dialing Extensions and More)

Sometimes you might need to have an extension or additional code after one or more of your numbers.
Adding a "Pause" in the dial string will do just that. To add a "Pause" just touch the "**+*#**" key at the bottom left of the dial pad. The "Pause" will be displayed as a "comma." When the phone number is dialed, the comma will turn into a 2-second pause.

TIP: To add more time, simply insert another pause. If you needed a 6-second pause, you would put three commas together ",,,"

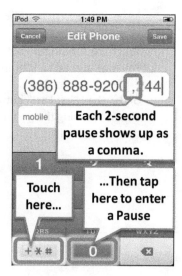

Each 2-second pause shows up as a comma.

Touch here...

...Then tap here to enter a Pause

Changing the Default Ringtone for a Contact

Tap the "**Ringtone**" tab under the phone number to change the default ringtone for a contact. The "Ringtone" options included the built in ringtones on the iPhone as well as any ringtones you might have purchased or created – see page 123 for more information.

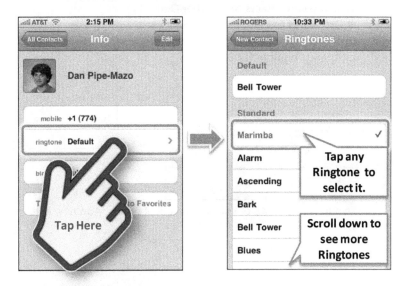

Adding Email Address and Web Site

Touch the "**add new email**" tab and input the Email Address for your contact. You can also touch the tab under the email address and select whether this is a home, work or other email address.

Under the Edit Email options you will also see places to add additional phone numbers, Anniversary dates or custom labels – for user-defined information. You might also see a line that says PIN. If you are a BlackBerry user and have synced your contacts from either Outlook or Entourage or Mac Mail you might see the PIN line available. A PIN is a unique identifying number for BlackBerry devices.

To add the Website of your Contact, just touch "**Add new URL**" and input the web site.

Adding the Address

Under the URL tab is the tab for adding the address. Input the Street, City, State and Zip Code. You can also specify the Country and whether this is a home or work address.

When you are done, just touch the "**Save**" button in the upper right hand corner.

Adding a Photo to Contacts (Picture Caller ID and More)

From the "**Add new Contact**" screen we have been working in, just touch the "**Add Photo**" box next to the "**First Last**" tab.

You then have the option to "**Choose an Existing Photo**" or "**Cancel.**" Choose "**Choose Existing Photo**."

Specify in which Photo Album the picture is located and touch the corresponding tab. When you see the picture you want to use, just touch it.

You will notice that the top and bottom become "grayed out" and that the picture can be manipulated by moving it, pinching to "Zoom in" or "Zoom out" and then arranged in the picture window.

Once the Picture is sitting where you want it, just touch "**Set Photo**" and that picture will be set for the Contact.

Searching Your Contacts

Let's say you need to find a specific phone number or email address. Just start your "Contacts" icon as we did above. There should be a "Search Box" at the top of the window of your "Contacts."

TIP: If you are somewhere in the middle or bottom of your contact list, you can quickly get back to the "Search" window in one of two ways: (Method 1) The fastest way is to tap the little magnifying glass above the letter "A" in the alphabet on the right side, or (Method 2) to hold your finger on the alphabet on the right until it becomes highlighted in gray -- then drag your finger to the very top to see the Search window. Sometimes, you will find that just tapping the little magnifying glass may result in inadvertently tapping the blue plus sign to add a new contact, so you may find that Method 2 is more reliable.

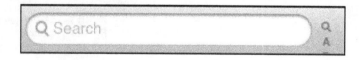

If not, just touch the small magnifying glass above the letter "A" and the search window will pop up.

Input the first few letters of any of these three searchable fields:

- First Name
- Last Name
- Company Name

The iPhone will begin to 'filter' and display only those contacts who match the letters typed.

TIP: To further narrow the search, hit the "space" key and type a few more letters.

When you see the correct name, just touch the name and that individuals contact information will appear.

Quickly Jump to a Letter by Tapping and Sliding on the Alphabet

If you hold your finger on the alphabet on the right edge of the phone and drag it up or down, you

Search by "Flicking"

If you don't want to manually input letters, you can just move your finger and "Flick" from the bottom up and you will see your Contacts move quickly on the screen. Just continue to Flick or Scroll until you see the name you are looking for. Just touch the name and the contact information will appear.

Search using "Groups"

If you have synced your iPhone with your PC or Mac and you have your contacts sorted by "Groups" on the computer, those groups will be synced to your iPhone. Just touch the "Groups" tab at the top left of the "All Contacts" window and select which group (if you have more than one) you would like to search within.

Adding Contacts from Emails

Often times, you might receive an Email and realize that the contact is not in your Address book. Adding a new "Contact" from an email is easy.

Open the Email from the Contact you wish to add to your Contact list. In the "**From**" field of the Email, just touch the name of the "Sender" next to the "From:" tag.

If the "Sender" is not already in your address book, you will be taken to a screen that will ask you whether you want to add that Email Address to an "existing" contact or "Create a New Contact."

If you select "**Create a New Contact**" you will be taken to the same screen to add a new contact as we did above.

If you would like to add this Email address to an existing contact. For example, if this is someone's personal email address and you already have an entry with their work email, then you would select "**Add to Existing Contact**" and choose the correct person. Then, you will have to give this email address a tag, like 'work' or 'personal.'

Sending a Picture to a Contact

If you want to send a picture to a contact, you will need to do that from either the Camera Icon (see page 134) or from the Photos Icon (see page 274).

Sending an Email Message from Contacts

Since many of the core Icons (Contacts, Phone, Mail and Messages) are fully integrated, one Icon can easily trigger another. So, if you want to send an Email to one of your Contacts, open the Contact, tap their Email address and your Mail Icon will launch and you can compose and send an email message to this person.

Start your "Contacts" by touching the "Contacts" icon. Either "Search" or "Flick" through your contacts until you find the contact for which you are searching. (See page 248 for Contact searching tips.)

work **martin@blackberrymadesi...**

In the contact information, touch the email address of the Contact you would like to use.

You will see that the "Mail" program launched automatically with the Contact's name in the "To" field of the Email. Type and send the message.

Mapping Your Contacts (Google Maps)

One of the very cool things about the iPhone is the integration with Google Maps. This is very evident in the Contacts Icon. Let's say you want to map a home or work address of any contact in your address book. In the old days (pre-iPhone) you would have to use "Google" or use "MapQuest" or some other program and laboriously re-type the address information. Very time consuming -- Not so on the iPhone.

Simply open the Contact as you did above. This time, touch the "Address" at the bottom of the Contact information.

> work **25 forest view way**
> **Ormand beach FL 32174**

Immediately, your Maps Icon (which is powered by Google Maps) will load and drop a "Push Pin" at the exact location of the Contact. The Address will appear in a tab above the Push Pin.

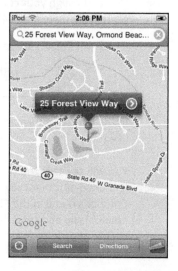

Touch tab on the top of the push-pin to get to the "Info" Screen.

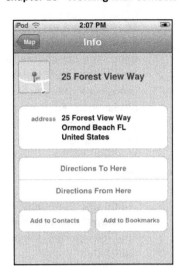

Now you may select "Directions To Here" or "Directions From Here."

Then, type the correct start or end address and touch the "Route" button in the lower right hand corner. If you decide you don't want the directions, just tap the "Clear" button in the top left.

ADD TO CONTACTS:
If you had just typed the address in your Maps icon (not clicked in from your contact list), you might want to touch "**Add to Contacts**" to add this address.

TIP: To return to your "Contact" information, you will need to tap the "Home" button and then tap "**Contacts**" again.

Contact Settings and Options

Like other settings, the Contact options are located in the "Settings" Icon.

Touch the "**Settings**" icon and scroll down to "**Mail, Contacts, Calendars**" and touch the tab.

Scroll Down and you will see Contacts and two options underneath. To change the "Sort Order" just touch the "**Sort Order**" tab and select whether you want your Contacts sorted with First or Last name first.

You may want to change how your Contacts are displayed. Here is where you get it done - you can choose "First, Last" or "Last, First." Tap the **"Display Order"** tab and choose whether you want your Contact displayed in "First" name or "Last" name order. Tap the **"Mail"** button in the upper left corner to save your settings changes.

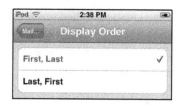

Searching for GAL Contacts

Open your "Contacts" App as you normally would. Touch the "**Groups**" button in the top left hand corner. Then look for the "Directories" tab at the bottom of your "Group" list and touch it.

Contact Troubleshooting

Sometimes, your Contacts Icon might not work the way you are hoping. If you don't see all your contacts, review the steps in the iTunes chapter (page 92) on how to "Sync" with your Address Book Application – make sure you have selected "All Groups" in the settings in iTunes.

TIP: If you are syncing with another Contact application (e.g. Contacts in Gmail), make sure you have selected the option closest to "All Contacts."

When GAL ("Global Address List") Contacts Don't Show up (For Microsoft Exchange Users)

First, make sure you are connected to either the cellular network and see the "E" or "3G" in your wireless status bar on the top of your iPhone or you are connected to Wi-Fi network – see page 197.

Next, check your Exchange setting and verify that you have setup the correct server and login information. To verify, go to the "**Settings**" icon and then scroll to and touch "**Mail, Contacts and Calendar**."

Find your Exchange account from the list and touch it to look at the settings.

You may need to contact your Technical Support to make sure your Exchange settings are correct.

Chapter 17:
Your Calendar

Manage your Busy Life on your iPhone

The "Calendar" App is a powerful and easy to use application that really helps you manage your appointments, keep track of what you have to do, set reminder alarms and even accept Meeting Initiations (for Enterprise users).

Today's Day and Date Shown on Calendar Icon

The Calendar Icon is usually right on your iPhone Home Screen. You will quickly see that your Calendar Icon changes to show today's date and day of the week. The icon to the right shows that it is a Tuesday and the 9th of the month.

TIP: If you use your Calendar often, you might want to think about "pinning" or moving it to the Bottom Dock – learn how on page 157.

Syncing or Sharing Your Calendar(s) with your iPhone

If you maintain a calendar on your computer, or on a web site, like a Google Calendar, you can synchronize or share that calendar with your iPhone either using iTunes and your sync cable or by setting up a wireless synchronization (see page 92).

After you setup the calendar sync, all of your computer calendar appointments will be synced into your iPhone calendar automatically based on your Sync settings. If you use iTunes to sync with your calendar (e.g. Microsoft Outlook, Entourage or Apple's iCal), your appointments will be transferred or synced every time you connect your iPhone to your computer.

If you use another method to sync (e.g. Mobile Me, Google Sync, or similar) this sync is wireless and automatic and will most likely happen without you having to do anything after the initial setup process.

Viewing your Schedule and Getting Around

The default view for the Calendar is your "Day" view. It will show you at a glance any upcoming appointments for your day. Appointments are shown in your calendar. If you happen to have several different calendars, like "Work" and "Home," that you have setup on your computer, you will see these as separate colors on your iPhone calendar.

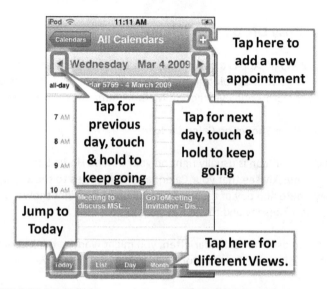

MOVE DAY AT A TIME:
If you tap the triangles next to the Day / Date at the top, you move forward or backward a day.

TIP: Press and hold the triangles to keep moving forward or backward.

CHANGING VIEWS:
Use the "List," "Day," and "Month" buttons at the bottom.

JUMP TO TODAY:
Use the "Today" button a the bottom.

Calendar Day, List and Month Views

Your iPhone comes with three views: Day, List and Month as shown below. You can switch views by tapping the name of the view at the bottom of the screen.

DAY VIEW:

When you start your calendar, the default view is usually the "Day" view. This allows you to quickly see everything you have scheduled for the day. At the bottom of the calendar are buttons to change the view.

LIST VIEW or "AGENDA" VIEW:

Touch the "List" view button at the bottom and you can see a list of your appointments coming up. Depending on how much you have scheduled, you could see the next day or even in the next week worth of scheduled events.

MONTH VIEW:
Touch the "Month" view and you can see a layout of the full month. Days with appointments have a small dot in them. The current day will show up highlighted in blue. Today's appointments will be at the bottom of the Month view.

GO TO NEXT MONTH: Tap the triangle to the right of the month name.

GO TO PREVIOUS MONTH: Tap the triangle to the left of the month name.

To look on another day while in Month view, just touch a different date. To return to "Today" just touch the

"Today" tab at the bottom left.

To advance days in "Day View," just touch the arrows to either side of the date.

NOTE: While you can "scroll" in the calendar, counter to what you might think, you cannot "swipe" through your days.

Working with Several Calendars (Different Colors)

Your iPhone Calendar can keep various calendars. The number of calendars you see depends on how you setup your synchronization using iTunes or other sync methods (see page 92). In the example below, we have categorized personal appointments in our "Home" calendar, and have our work appointments in a separate "Work" calendar.

In the appointments in my calendar, I have my "Home" calendar appointments showing up in Red and my "Work" appointments in Orange. When you set up your Sync settings, you were able to specify which calendars you wanted to Sync with your iPhone. Take a look back on Page 92 for more information.

HOW TO CHANGE THE COLORS?
You will need to change the color of the calendar in the program on your computer which is synced to your iPhone. Then the colors will change on your iPhone.

HOW TO ADD A NEW CALENDAR?
It's a 2-step process to add a new calendar to sync with your iPhone:
Step 1: Setup that new calendar on your computer's calendar program
Step 2: Adjust your sync (see page 92) to make sure this new calendar syncs to your iPhone.

VIEWING ONLY ONE CALENDAR:
To view just one calendar at a time, tap the "Calendars" button at the top and select only the calendar you wish to see.

Adding New Calendar Appointments / Events

You can easily add new appointments right on your iPhone and they will be synced (or shared with) your computer the next time the sync takes place.

Adding a New Appointment

Your instinct will most likely be to try to "Touch" the screen at a particular time to set an appointment; unfortunately, this is not how setting appointments work. (You may have been used to this from another Smartphone like a BlackBerry or a Palm.)

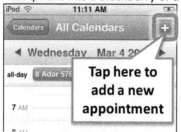

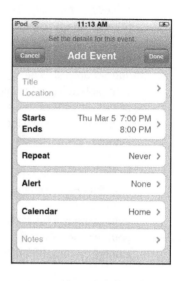

To add a new calendar event from any Calendar view, tap the blue "+" at the top right corner of the screen. The "**Add Event**" screen will now show.

First, touch the first box marked "**Title/Location.**"

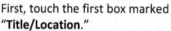

Type in a title for the event and the location (optional). We might type "Meet with Martin" as the title and the location would be "Office."

Or, we might choose to type "Lunch with Martin" and then choose a very expensive restaurant. Touch the blue "**Done**" or "**Save**" button in the upper right corner to return to the Add Event screen.

Touch the Starts / Ends tab to adjust the
event timing.

TO CHANGE THE START TIME:
Touch the "**Starts**" field to highlight it in
blue. Then, move the rotating dials at the
bottom to reflect the correct date and
start time of the appointment.

TO CHANGE THE END TIME:
Touch "**Ends**" field and use the rotating
dials.
TO SET AN ALL-DAY EVENT:
Touch the switch next to "**All-day**" to set it
to "**YES**."

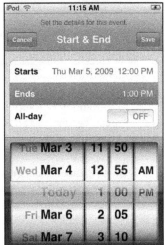

Recurring Events (Repeat Events) and Alert (Alarm)

Some of your appointments happen every day, week or month at the same time. If the appointment you are scheduling is a repeating or 'recurring' appointment, just touch the "Repeat" tab and then select the correct option from the list.

Touch "**Done**" or "**Save**" to get back to the main Event screen.

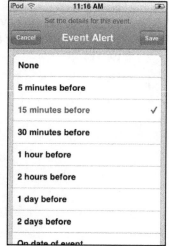

Alerts can be useful – an audible reminder of an upcoming appointment can certainly keep you from forgetting an important event.

Just touch the "**Alert**" tab and then select the option for a reminder alarm. You can have no alarm at all or set a time from 5 minutes before all the way to 2 days before – whatever works best for you.

Touch "**Done**" or "**Save**" to get back to the main Event screen.

ADDING A SECOND ALERT:
After you add one Alert, you are given the option to add a second (optional) alert.

This can be really useful if you need a second reminder to be sure you do not miss the event. For example, if you needed to pick up your kids at the bus stop, you might want one alert 15 minutes ahead of time, then one final alert 5 minutes ahead of time, so you can be absolutely certain that you don't miss the pickup.

Choosing Which Calendar to Use

If you use more than one Calendar in Outlook, Entourage, iCal or other program and you sync your iPhone with that program, you will have various calendars available to you.

Touch the "Calendar" tab to see all your calendars. Tap the calendar you want to use for this particular event. Usually, the calendar selected is the last one you selected for the previous event you scheduled on your iPhone.

I scheduled a new event on the wrong calendar, how can I switch it?
You will notice that whey you edit the calendar event on your iPhone, you will not have the option to switch the calendar on which the event is scheduled. In order to change the scheduled calendar on your iPhone, you will need to delete the original event and schedule a new event on the different calendar.

Adding Notes to Calendar Events

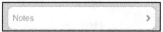

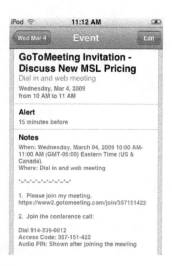

If you want to add some notes to this calendar event, tap "Notes" and type a few notes.

TIP: If this is a meeting somewhere new, you could type or copy/paste (requires 3.0 software) some driving directions.

TIP: If this is a scheduled conference call or call with someone, just type their phone number in the Notes field. Then you can call directly from the calendar without having to look up the number when the calendar alarm rings.

Dialing the Phone from Your Calendar

You can quickly dial the phone from any calendar event as long as you type the phone number in the NOTES field in the calendar event.

ADDING PHONE NUMBERS TO NOTES ON CALENDAR EVENTS

If this is a scheduled call or conference call, type the call number in the NOTES field.

You can enter it in any of these formats:

386-111-2222
3861112222
(386)111-2222
386 111 2222

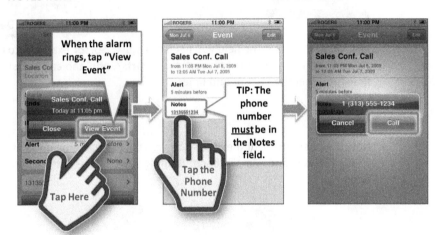

Editing Appointments

Sometimes, the details of an appointment may change and need to be adjusted. Fortunately, this is an easy task on your iPhone.

First, locate the appointment that needs to change and touch it. In the upper right hand corner, you will see the "Edit" button. Touch "**edit**" and you return to the appointment details screen.

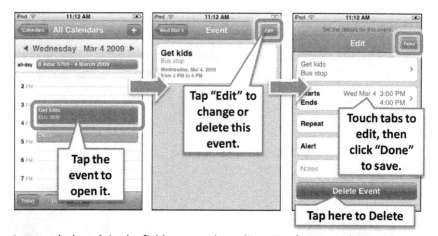

Just touch the tab in the field you need to adjust. So, for example, to change the time of this appointment, touch the "**Starts/Ends**" tab and adjust the time for either the start or end times.

Deleting an Event

Notice at the bottom of the "Edit" screen, you also have the option to "Delete" this event. Simply touch "**Delete Event**" at the bottom of the screen.

Meeting Invitations

For those who work in the "Enterprise" world, use Microsoft Exchange or use Outlook or Entourage regularly, meeting invitations become a way of life. You receive a meeting invitation in your email, you accept the invitation and then the appointment gets put in your calendar.

On your iPhone, you will see that invitations that you "Accept" get put right into your calendar.

If you touch on the Meeting Invitation in your calendar you can see all the details that you need – the dial in number, meeting ID or any other details that might be in the invitation.

NOTE: You can accept meeting invitations on your iPhone, but you cannot create them. They will transfer automatically from Entourage or Outlook if you have iTunes set to Sync with those programs.

Calendar Options

There are just a few options to adjust in your Calendar found in the Settings Icon. Just touch Settings from your Home Screen.

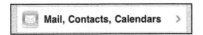

Scroll down to "Mail, Contacts, Calendars" and touch the tab. Scroll down to Calendars and you will see three options. The first option is a simple switch to be notified of New Invitation Alerts – if you receive any meeting invites, it is good to keep this set in the default "ON" position.

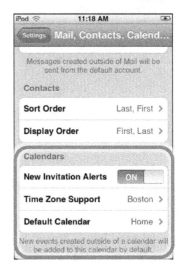

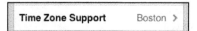

Next, you can choose your time zone support. It should reflect your "Home" settings from when you set up your iPhone – see page 43. If you are traveling, however and want to adjust your appointments for a different time zone, you can change this to any other city you would like.

Changing the Default Calendar

We mentioned earlier that you can have multiple calendars displayed on your iPhone.   This option allows you to choose which calendar will be your "Default" calendar.

That means that when you go to schedule every new appointment, this calendar will be selected by default.

If you wish to use a different calendar – say, your "Work" calendar, you can just change that when you actually set the appointment as shown on page 259.

Chapter 18:
Working with Pictures (Photos)

Photos on your iPhone

Due in large part to the beautiful screen on the iPhone, viewing pictures is a joy. Using the touch screen interface makes navigating, zooming and manipulating your photos lots of fun.

Launching the Photos Icon

If you like using your "Photos" Icon, you might want to place it in your Bottom Dock for easy access (see page 157).
To get started with photos, touch the "Photos" Icon.

The first screen shows you your Photo Albums. These were created when you set up you iPhone and Synced with iTunes. On page 98, we showed you how to choose which photos to Sync with your iPhone. As you make changes to the library on your computer, they will be automatically updated on your iPhone.

Choose a Library

From the Photo Albums page, touch one of the library tabs to show the photos in that Album. We touched the "Photo Library" collection and immediately the screen changed to show us thumbnails of the pictures in this library.

Tap and drag your finger up and down to view all the pictures. You can flick up or down to quickly move throughout the album.

Working with Individual Pictures

Once we locate the picture we want to view, we just tap on it to view it. The picture then loads into the screen.

NOTE: Usually, your pictures will not take up the full screen on your iPhone especially if they were shot in "Landscape Mode."

TIP: The picture to the right was shot in "Landscape Mode," so to see it in full screen you will have to tilt your iPhone on its side.

Moving Between Pictures

The "Swipe" gesture shown on page 26 is used to move from one picture to the next. Just "Swipe" your finger left or right across the screen, and you can move through your pictures.

TIP: Drag your finger slowly to slowly move through the picture library.

When you read the end of that particular library, just "Tap" the screen once and you will see a tab in the upper left hand corner that says "Photo Library." Touch that tab and you will return to the thumbnail page of that particular album.

To get back to your main Photo Album page, just touch the tab that reads "Photo Albums" in the top left hand corner.

Using the Arrows to Move Between Pictures

Instead of swiping left and right to move between your pictures, you can bring up the soft key controls at the bottom of the screen. To do this simply "Tap" the screen once. Tap it again to make the soft keys disappear.

The arrow pointing to the right is for advancing forward to the next picture in the library and the arrow to the left is for moving back to the previous picture in the library.

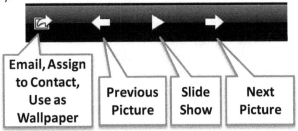

Zooming in and Out of Pictures

As described in the "Getting Started" section of the book, there are two ways to Zoom in and out of pictures on your iPhone: "Double Tapping" (page 28) and "Pinching" (page 29).

Double Tapping

As the name describes, this is a quick "Double tap" on the screen to "Zoom in" on the picture. You will be zoomed in on the spot where you double tap.

See page 28 for more help on Double-Tapping.

To "Zoom out" just "Double Tap" once more.

Pinching

Also described in the "Getting Started" chapter on page 29, "Pinching" is a much more precise form of zoom. While "Double Tapping" only zooms in or out to one set level, "Pinching" really allows you to "Zoom" in or out just a little bit or quite a bit.

To "Pinch," hold your thumb and forefinger close together and then slowly (while touching the screen) separate them – making the picture larger. To "Zoom in" just start with your thumb and forefinger apart and move them together.

NOTE: Once you have activated the "Zoom" by either method, you will not be able to "Swipe" through your pictures until you return the picture back to its standard size.

Viewing a Slide Show

You can view the pictures in your Photo Album as a "Slide Show" if you would like. Just "Tap" the screen once to bring up the on-screen soft keys. The center icon looks like a "Play" symbol – just touch once to start the slide show. You can start the slide show from either the "Photo Library" screen of from any Picture you are viewing.

To end the slide show, just tap the screen. You can adjust the duration of each picture as well as the Transition, Repeat and Shuffle settings.

Using a Picture as Your iPhone Wallpaper

Your Wallpaper is the picture that comes on as soon as you "Wake" or turn on your iPhone. On page 162 we showed you how to change your Wallpaper. You can always set your wallpaper to be one of your pictures from your collection.

Setting Picture as Wallpaper

When viewing a picture that you would want to use as your "Wallpaper," just tap the screen until the bottom row of soft keys appears. Tap the left-most icon.

Use as Wallpaper

Tap the "Use as Wallpaper" button. On the next screen, you are asked to "Move and Scale" the picture. Tap and drag your finger to move the picture and use the pinch motion to zoom in or out (see page 29) so it looks best in the space provided.

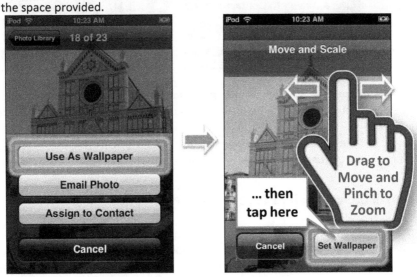

When you are sure of how the picture looks, touch the "**Set Wallpaper**" button to set the picture as your wallpaper.

Emailing a Picture

As long as you have an active network connection, either with the EDGE ("E") or 3G ("3G") cellular networks, or a Wi-Fi Connection (page 197) you can send any picture in your photo collection via email. Tap the Options button as you did above – the one furthest to the left of the bottom row of soft keys. If you don't see the icons, tap the screen once.

Choose the "**Email Photo**" option and your "Mail" program will automatically launch.

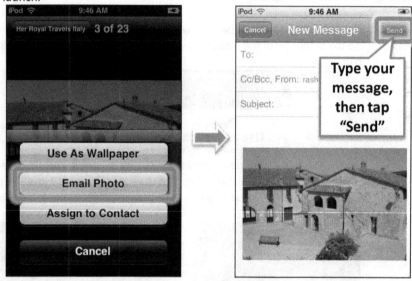

Touch the "To" field as you did in the Email Chapter on page and select the contact to receive the picture. Tap the blue "+" button to add a contact.

Type in a subject and a message and then touch "**Send**" in the upper right hand corner – that's all there is to it.

Email, Copy or Delete Several Pictures At Once

If you have several pictures you want to email, copy or delete at one time, you need to do it from the thumbnail view. NOTE: The copy function requires that you have installed version 3.0 of the iPhone software. (Learn how to upgrade to 3.0 on page 364).

NOTE: At publishing time, you could only "Share" or Email a maximum of five pictures. This may change with future software.

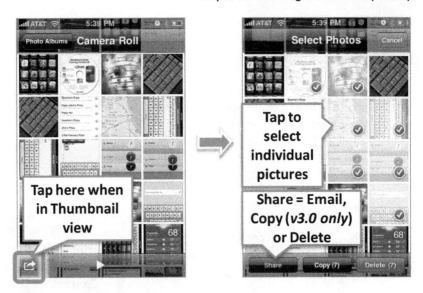

Assign Picture to a Contact

On page 246, we talked about adding a picture when editing a contact. You can also find a picture that you like and choose to assign it to a contact from the "Photos" Icon. First, find the photo you want to use.

As we did with Wallpaper, and Emailing the Photo, tap the Options button – the one furthest to the left of the bottom row of soft keys. If you don't see the icons, tap the screen once.

With the picture open, tap the screen to bring up the icons at the bottom of the screen. Activate the Photo "Options" – the icon on the bottom left.

Touch the "**Assign to Contact**" button.

Choose "Assign to Contact"

You will see your "Contacts" on the screen. You can either perform a search using the search bar at the top or just scroll through your contacts. Remember, if you don't see the search bar, just touch the small magnifying glass above the letter "A." (See page 248 for Contact searching tips.)

Once you find the contact to which you would like to add the picture, touch the name.

You will then see the "Move and Scale" screen. Tap and drag the picture to move it and use the pinch to zoom in or out.

When you have it just as you want, touch the "**Set Photo**" button to assign the picture to that contact.

NOTE: You will return to your Photo Library – not the Contact. If you want to check that the picture did get set to your contact you will need to exit the Photo Icon and start the Contact Icon and then search for that contact.

Deleting a Picture

Why are there some pictures I cannot delete from my iPhone (Trash Can Icon is missing)?

You will notice that the "Trash can" icon is not visible for any photo that is synced from iTunes. For these pictures, you can only delete them from your computer library. Then they will delete from your iPhone.

When you are looking through picture in your "Camera Roll" (which is not Synced with iTunes, but comprised of pictures you take on your Camera, receive and save from an Email, or download from the web). You will have a "Trash" can icon in the bottom icon bar. This "Trash can" icon does not appear when you are viewing pictures from your "Photo Library" or other "synced" albums.

If you don't see the bottom row of icons, tap the photo once to activate them. Then tap the "Trash Can" icon. You will be prompted with the option to "Delete" the picture.

Touch "**Delete**" and the picture will be deleted from your iPhone.

Downloading Pictures from Web Sites

We have shown you how pictures can be transferred from your Computer to your iPhone as well as saved from Emails. You can also download and save pictures right from the Web onto your iPhone.

Respect Copyright Laws: We strongly encourage you to respect image copyright laws as you download and save images from the web. Unless the web site says "free" image, you should check with the web site owner before downloading and saving any pictures.

Find a Web Site with a Picture you wish to Download

The iPhone makes it easy to copy and save images from web sites. This can be handy when you are looking for a new image to use as Wallpaper on your iPhone.

 First, Tap your Safari web browser icon and type a search "iPhone Wallpaper" to locate a few sites that might have some interesting wallpapers. (see our Chapter on Web Browsing for help on page 201)

Once you navigate to the picture you want to download and save, tap and hold it to bring up a new menu of options. You will see "Save Image" (and if you have version 3.0 installed, you will also see "Copy"). Choose "Save Image" to save the image to the "Camera Roll" in your Photos Icon.

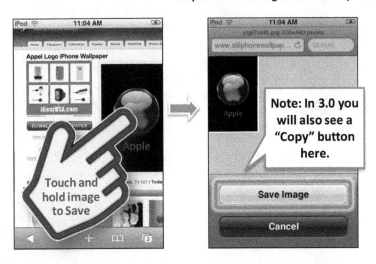

Touch your "Photo" App icon and you should see the picture in the "Camera Roll" or "Saved Images" Albums.

Send Picture as MMS - Multi-Media Message

iPhone 3.0 New Photo Feature

With the new 3.0 OS, you will have the option of also sending your pictures via MMS (Multi Media Messaging) to any capable Mobile Phone. Look on page 136 for the details.

Adjusting Slideshow Options for Photos

 Like other icons, you will need to change options in the Settings icon. Start your "Settings" Icon from the Home Screen.

Scroll down to the "Photos" tab and touch the screen. You will then see the various options you can adjust.

There are four Slideshow options you can adjust. To adjust how long each slide is played for, just touch the "Play Each Slide For" tab. You can choose a range between 2 and 20 seconds.

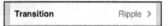

Touch the "Transition" tab and you can choose among five possible transitions. A transition is the way the iPhone moves from one picture to the next in a Slideshow. Some of the transitions like "Cube" and "Ripple" are very cool effects as the pictures move from one to the other.

If you want pictures to "Repeat" in a
Slideshow, just move the **"Repeat"** switch
to **"ON."**

| Repeat | OFF |
| Shuffle | OFF |

If you want the pictures to move in an
order different from the way they are
listed, just choose **"Shuffle"** and just like
the "Shuffle" command on the music
player, the pictures will play in a random
order.

Chapter 19:
Maps powered by Google Maps

Getting Started with Maps

The beauty of the iPhone is that the programs are just meant to work with one another. We have already seen how your Contacts are linked to the "Maps" Icon.

The Maps Icon is powered by Google Maps - the leader in mobile mapping technology. With "Maps" you can locate your position, get directions, search for things nearby, see traffic and much more.

Simply touch the "Map" icon to get started.

Determining your Location

When you start the "Map" program, you can immediately have maps start at your current location. Tap the small circle in the lower

Find my
Current
Location

left hand corner.

Maps will ask to use your current location – just touch "**OK**" or "**Don't Allow**."

We suggest choosing "**OK**" to make it much easier to find directions from, or to, your current location.

Changing the Map View: Map, Satellite, Hybrid and List

The "Default" view for "Maps" is a basic map view with generic background
and streets shown with their names. Maps can also show you a Satellite view
or a combination of Satellite and regular Map view called a "**Hybrid**" view.
LIST VIEW: If you have just searched for something or generated a list of turn-
by-turn directions, you can touch "**List View**" to see that list.

To see the "Viewing" Options

Touch the "**Map View**" button in the lower right hand corner. You will notice
that "Map" is the darkened button. If I touch "**Satellite**," my view will change
to a Satellite view of the terrain.

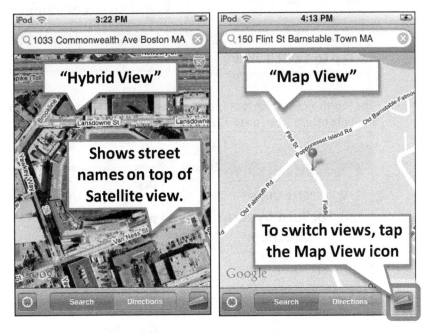

To change to a "**Hybrid**" view, touch the "**Map View**" button once more and
then touch the "**Hybrid**" button.

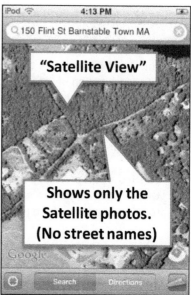

The fourth view, which is only available when you have done a search with multiple results (like "pizza 32174") or have asked for directions.

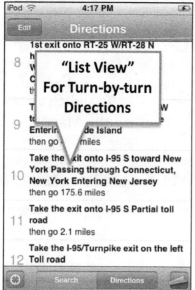

Checking Traffic

Your "Maps" program does have the
ability to check traffic along the way.
Just touch the **"Map View"** button in
the lower right hand corner and then
select the **"Show Traffic"** button from
the options shown.

On a highway, if there is a traffic situation,
you will usually see "Yellow" instead of
green – sometimes, the yellow might be
"flashing" to alert you to a traffic situation.

Traffic will be shown using colors to
indicate the speed that traffic is moving:

> Green = 50 MPH or more
> Yellow = 25 – 50 MPH
> Red = Less than 25 MPH
> Gray = no traffic data is currently
> available

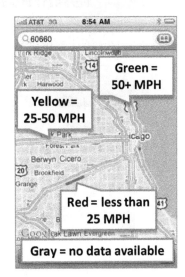

Search for Any Location, Local Businesses, Theaters, Plumbers, More

If your location cannot be determined by tapping the "My Location" button, or you want to map a specific address, city or other point of interest, touch the "Search" bar at the top of the program.

Type in your address, point of interest, or town and state you would like to map on your iPhone.

GOOGLE MAPS SEARCH TIPS
Enter just about anything in the search:
- First Name, Last Name or Company Name (to match your Contacts)
- 123 Main Street, City (Some or all of a street address)
- Orlando Airport (find an airport)
- Plumber, Painter, Roofer (any part of a business name or trade)
- Golf courses + city (find local golf courses)
- Movies + city or zip/postal code (find local movie theaters)
- Pizza 32174 (Search for local pizza restaurants in zip code 32174)
- 95014 (Zip Code - Apple Computer Headquarters in California, USA)
- N2L 3W8 (Postal Code for RIM - BlackBerry Headquarters in Canada)

To use numbers, for street addresses, tap the "123" key on the keyboard. For letters, touch the "ABC" to switch back to a letter keyboard,

Mapping Options Once Address or Addresses are Mapped

Now that your address is on the "Map" screen, there are a number of options available to you. Touch the Blue Arrow next to the address to see some of these.

You can get directions to that location or get Directions from that location by touching the appropriate button on the screen. You can also Add the address to your Contacts or add the Map to your Mapping Bookmarks for future reference.

Bookmarking Location

Bookmarking your location is a great way to make it easy to locate it again when you need it quickly. Touch the "Blue" arrow next to the address and then touch "**Add to Bookmarks**."

Edit the Bookmark name to make is short and recognizable - in this case, I will edit the address to simply say "Home." When you are done, just touch "**Save**" in the top left corner.

TIP: You can 'search' for bookmark names in the same way you search for contact names in your Contacts List.

Add Location to Contacts

If you wanted to add the location you mapped to a Contact in your

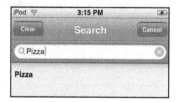

"Contacts," you would select "**Add to Contacts**."

Then you are presented with the option to either "**Create a New Contact**" or "**Add to an Existing Contact**."

If you choose "**Add to Existing Contact**," then you will scroll through or search your contacts and select a name. The address will automatically be added to that contact.

Searching for Things (Stores, Restaurants, Hotels, Movies, Anything) Around My Location

Let's say, now that we are on a map of our location. Maybe we just hit the 'My Location' button in the lower left corner or typed an address). We want to find some pizza to eat nearby. With our location on the screen, we just tap on the search bar and type in what we want to find - like "Pizza."

The closest Pizza restaurant to our current location will be in the center of the screen with a blue arrow next to it.

All the other (unnamed) red push pins are other Pizza restaurants. To see the name of another red dot, touch it.

Zoom in or out by double-tapping or using your two fingers to "pinch open" or "pinch closed" (learn more about zooming on page 29).

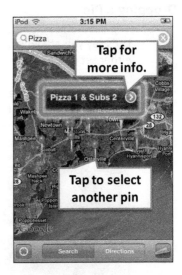

Just as with any mapped red dot, when we touch the blue arrow, we can see all the details, and even the pizza restaurant's phone number, address and its web site.

To order pizza and have it delivered, simply tap the phone number.

If we wanted directions to there, we would just touch "**Directions to Here**" and a route would be instantly calculated.

Zooming In and Out

You can zoom in and out in the familiar way of "Double Tapping" and "Pinching." To Zoom in by Double Tapping, just double tap on the screen as you would in a Web page or Picture. (See pages 28 and 29)

Dropping a Pin

Let's say you are looking at the map and you find something you would like to either set as a bookmark or as a destination.

In this example, we are zooming and looking around greater Boston and we stumble upon Fenway Park and decide it would be a great thing to add to our Bookmarks.

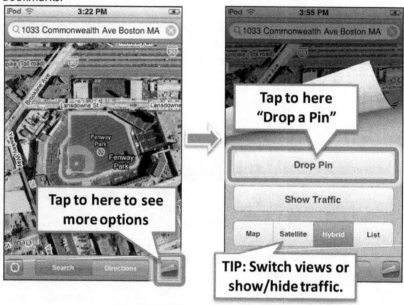

Tap the "Menu Icon" (looks like a page being back page) and select "**Drop Pin**" from the options listed. We can then "Drag" the pin by touching and holding it. We move it right onto Fenway Park.

How can you find the street address of any location on the map?

When you "Drop a Pin," Google Maps will show you the street address. This is great if you know a location by looking at Satellite view or Hybrid view, but need to get the actual street address.

Now, I just touch the "Blue" arrow next to my Purple Pin and choose "**Add to Bookmarks**" at the bottom.

We can also **"Remove the Pin"**, **"Add a Bookmark"** or get directions by touching blue arrow in the pop-up window above the map to see the next screen.

 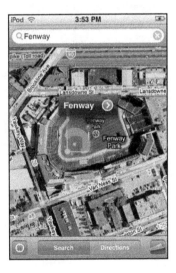

We should rename the bookmark so it is easier to remember. The next time we do a search of our bookmarks, Fenway will show up and we can immediately see it on the map. If we wanted to get directions, we would just touch the blue arrow and select **"Directions to Here."**

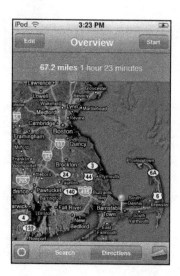

Getting Directions

Perhaps one of the most useful function of the "Maps" program is that you can easily find directions to or from any location. Let's say we want to use our current location and get directions to our friend Martin's house.

TAP THE MY LOCATION BUTTON FIRST
If you want to find directions to or from your current location, and you don't have to waste time typing your current address, make sure to locate yourself by tapping the "My Location" button ⬚ in the lower left corner. You may need to repeat it a few times until you see your blue dot on the screen.

We can do one of two things:
(1) Tap the "Directions" button at the bottom, or
(2) Touch the blue arrow as we did above and then select "**Directions from Here.**"

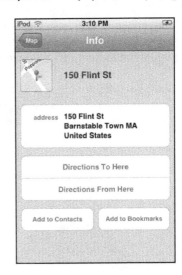

Choose "Start" or "End" location

In this example, we touched the Blue arrow next above the pin on the map and chose "**Get Directions from Here**." Now, we want to find Martin's address. Next to the "End" box, you will see a blue picture of the address book. We can touch the address book icon  and search for Martin's address or just type a few letters of Martin's first and last name it in the box to see his name appear below the search box. (See page 248 for tips on searching your Contacts List.)

Immediately, after selecting Martin's name from the Contact List, the routing screen takes me to an "Overview" screen.

A Green pushpin is dropped at my location and a Red one is dropped at my "End" location – in this case, Martin's house.

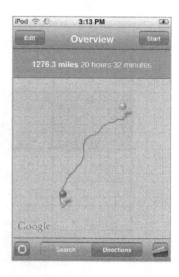

Looking at the Route

Touch the "Start" button in the upper right hand corner of the screen and the directions routing begins. Because this is a long trip, there are lots of pages to these directions (indicated by the number at the top of the screen - 28 steps.)

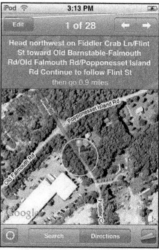

We can move the screen with our finger to look at the route, or we can just touch the arrows [←→] at the top to show the route in step-by-step snapshots.

Changing the Route

To change the route, we just touch the "Edit" button at the top left. We can change either the start or end location. This could be useful if we take a detour and want to input our new location in the start box.

"Maps" Options

 Currently the only setting that will affect your Maps icon is the **"Location Services"** which is critical for determining your "Current Location" in Maps.

Touch **"Settings"** from your home screen, then touch the **"General"** tab.

Once there, look about half-way down to the "Location services" switch. In order for the "Maps" App to approximate your locations you need this switch moved to the **"ON"** position.

NOTE: Keeping this switch in the **"ON"** location will reduce battery life by a small amount. If you never use Maps or care about your Location, then set this to **"OFF"** to save your battery life.

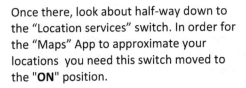
Set to "ON" so Maps can find your current location.

Chapter 20:
Eliminate Your Paper Notes
(Notes and Voice Memos)

You have a couple of choices on your iPhone, if you are running 3.0 software (or higher) to take notes: You can write notes using the Notes icon or take voice notes using the Voice Memo icon.

Working with Notes is something that will quickly become invaluable on your iPhone. Most of us have "Sticky" notes just about everywhere; on our desks, by the nightstand, on the computer…you get the idea.

"Notes" on the iPhone give you one, convenient place to keep your notes and simple "to do" lists. You can also keep simple lists like a grocery list or list for other stores like hardware and the pet store. Since you always have your iPhone with you, you can add items to these lists as soon as they occur to you and can be accessed and edited at any time.

Getting Started with Notes

Like all other applications, simply tap the "Notes" Icon to start it.

After starting the "Notes" App you see what looks like a typical yellow note pad.

NEED MORE CAPABLE, FLEXIBLE NOTES APP?

The Notes Icon is that comes with the iPhone is pretty basic and utilitarian. If you need a more robust notes application that you can sort, categorize, import items (PDF, Word, etc.), have folders, search, and more, you should check out the App Store on your iPhone. Do a search for 'notes' and you will find at least a dozen Notes related apps ranging from about $0.99 through $5.99 or more.

How are my notes sorted?

You will soon notice that all notes will be listed in reverse chronological order, with the most recently edited notes at the top and oldest at the bottom.

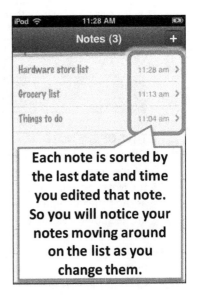

Each note is sorted by the last date and time you edited that note. So you will notice your notes moving around on the list as you change them.

The date that is shown is the last time and date that the particular note was edited, not when it was first created. So you will notice your notes moving around in order on the screen.

This sorting can be a good thing because your most recent (or frequently edited) notes will be right at the top.

Adding a New Note

To start a new "Note" touch the "+" sign in the upper right hand corner.

The notepad is blank and the keyboard pops up for you to begin typing.

TIP: Once you install 3.0 software (see page 364 for help), you can tilt your iPhone on its side to see the larger keyboard.

TITLE OF THE NOTE:

The first few words you type before you hit the "return" key will become Title of the Note. So think about what you want as the title and type that first. In the image shown, "Hardware store list" becomes the title of the note.

Put a new item on each line - tap "return" to go to the next line. When you are done, touch the "Done" button in the top

right hand corner.

Touch the "Notes" button in the top left hand corner to return to the main Notes screen.

Viewing or Editing your Notes

Your "Notes" appear in the list as tabs to touch. Touch the name of the note you wish to view or edit. The contents of the note are then displayed.

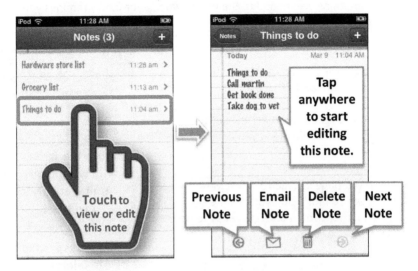

You can scroll in "Notes" as you do in any program. You will notice the Date and Time when the note was last edited appear the upper right hand corner.

When you are done reading the note, just touch the "Notes" button in the top left hand corner to return to the main "Notes" Screen.

To advance through multiple notes, just touch the arrows at the bottom of the screen. Touch the "forward" arrow. The page turns and you can see the next note. To go back, just hit the "Back" arrow.

Editing your Notes

You can very easily edit or change the contents of a note. For example, you might keep a "Grocery List" note and quickly edit it when you think of something else to add to the list (or when your family reminds you to get something from the store!)

Touch the "Grocery List" note, then touch the screen anywhere and the cursor moves to that spot for editing.

You can then type new lines of text, you may use the delete key to delete a word or a line.

If you have installed 3.0 software, (see page 364 for help), you use the select and then hit the backspace key to delete a block of text.

When done editing, touch the "**Done**" button.

Deleting Notes

To delete a "Note," tap it to open it from the main Notes screen and then touch the "trash can" icon at the bottom.

The iPhone prompts you to "Delete Note" or just "Cancel."

Emailing a Note

One of the very convenient features on "Notes" is the ability to email a note. Let's say we wrote a grocery note and wanted to email it to our spouse. From the text of the note, touch the small envelope icon at the bottom of the screen.

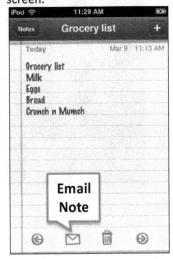 

Now we see the "Compose New Mail" screen with the subject as the title of the Note and the body of the message as the contents of the note. Address and send the note as you would any other email. Touch the "To" line of the

email, touch the "+" sign and find the contact I wish to use.

Voice Memos or Voice Notes

 Part of the new 3.0 Operating System is a new App called "Voice Memos." Just touch the "Voice Memos" icon to get started.

Recording a Voice Memo

Just touch the Voice Memo icon and you will see an old-fashioned looking microphone on the screen. Touch the "Red" record button in the lower left hand corner and just speak your message. When you are done, just touch the "Stop" button in the right hand corner – that's all there is to it.

Playing your Voice Memos

Just touch the "**Play**" button in the lower right hand corner and you can see all your Voice Memos. Just scroll through them and press the blue "Play" arrow to play the memo.

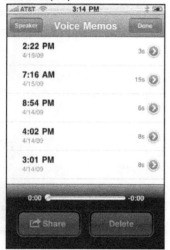 

Getting more Information and "Labeling" Memos

In the Voice Memo line, you will notice a blue arrow (not the "Play" button) to the far right. Touch that arrow and the details of the voice Memo will be displayed.

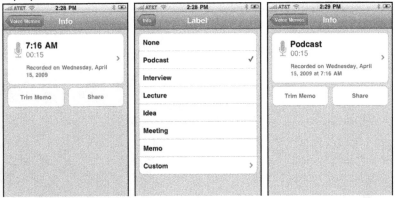

To assign a unique "Label" to the Memo (so you will remember later, exactly what it is) just touch the arrow to the right of the large window. You can then select one of the labels – I will cal this one a "Podcast" and then the name will change to reflect the new name.

If I wanted to give a "Custom" name to your voice memo, just touch "**Custom**" and type in a "Custom" name.

"Trimming" your Memos

You might find that your Memo is longer than it needs to be. From the Info screen you were in before, just select **"Trim Memo"** and touch the screen. Touch and hold either end of the slider and you will see the time of the memo on the screen.

To trim this Voice Memo to only contain the first 7 seconds, I just move the slider from the right so the time reflects 00:01 – 00:07.

Press the **"Play"** button at any time to listen to the "trimmed" section to make sure the memo plays the way your desire. Once you have the memo exactly edited to your liking, touch the yellow **"Trim Voice Memo"** button and the changes will be set.

"Sharing" your Memo

The new iPhone 3.0 OS allows you "Share" your voice memo. Just touch the **"Share"** button, either from the "Info" screen above or from the blue **"Share"** button in the main Voice Memos list.

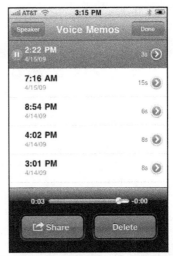

You have the choice of sending the Voice Memo via Email or MMS. If you choose MMS, the voice mail will look like a "Quicktime" Icon in the small bubble on the screen.

Chapter 21:
Clock, Calculator & Weather

The iPhone is very useful for a great number of things. Some of the most 'simple' things and apps are those you might find yourself using quite frequently.

You may want to see what time it is in London, Tokyo or any other city around the world. You might want a wake-up alarm clock. How about a count-down timer to tell you when the pasta is finished boiling or a stop watch to time how long it takes to get something done. All these can be done in the Clock Icon.

How about calculating the tip on your meal, or other simple, everyday calculations - what would 120 license of our Made Simple videos cost a company at $15.95 each? Use the calculator.

How about the weather for the next few days in your city, or any city in the world. Use the Weather Icon.

The World Time Clock

Touch the "Clock" icon to launch the Clock.

Immediately, you see the "World Clock" feature. Usually, the standard clock is for Cupertino, CA – but you can easily add to that or delete it.

Adding a New World Clock Entry

Touch the "+" sign  in the upper right hand corner and the keyboard will pop up. Type in the name of a City.

As you type, the iPhone will show you entries that match your letters. When you see the city you want, tap it to select it.

Once you do, the new City is automatically added to the "World Clock" list.

Re-Sorting or Deleting World Time Entries

Just touch the "Edit" button in the top left of the screen. You will notice that each entry now has a read "-" sign. When you touch the minus sign, it will rotate 90 degrees and a red "Delete" box will appear to the right.

Touch "**Delete**" and that particular World Clock Entry will no longer be in the list.

To Move a World Time entry, touch and

drag the three bars you see to the right of each entry.

Drop or let go of the entry when you have it in the correct location.

The Alarm Clock

The alarm clock feature is very flexible and powerful on the iPhone. You can easily set multiple alarms. For example, you might set an alarm to wake you up on weekdays, and a separate one on weekends. You can even set a separate alarm to wake you up from your Tuesday and Sunday afternoon nap at 3:00pm.

To get started, tap the "**Alarm**" clock in the lower row of soft keys.

If you have alarms set, they will be displayed. If there are no "Alarms" tap the "+" sign in the upper right hand corner to add a new one.

Adjust the time of the alarm by rotating the dials at the bottom of the screen.

If this is a one-time alarm, then leave the Repeat set at "**Never**." A "**Never**" repeating alarm will cause the alarm to automatically be set at "**OFF**" after it rings.

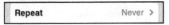

If the alarm does repeat, then adjust the "Repeating" function of the Alarm by touching the "**Repeat**" tab. Touch the days of the week you would like the Alarm to be active.

TIP: You may touch as many or as few days as you want.

Adjust the sound the alarm makes by touching the "**Sound**" tab and then choosing an alarm sound from the list.

SILENT ALARM: Set the Sound to "**None**" at the top of the list to have an on-screen silent alarm - no sound will be made.

Tap "**Back**" when you are done.

To enable the "Snooze" feature – make sure the "**Snooze**" Switch is in the default "**ON**" position. NOTE: The pre-set snooze time is 10 minutes and could not be changed as of the writing of this book.

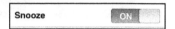

You can re-name your Alarm by touching the "**Label**" tab. The keyboard will launch and you can type in a new name for that particular alarm.

Give your alarm a name that is easy to recognize.

NOTE: if you want to use this feature to wake up in the morning, you will need to set an alarm for each day of the week following the procedure above.

Will an Alarm turn on my iPhone?

No. If your iPhone is completely powered-off (see page 36), the alarm will not turn it back on. However, if your iPhone is just in **Sleep Mode** (see page 38), then your alarms will ring just fine.

Using the Stopwatch

The iPhone comes with a built in stopwatch which can be a very handy feature. Just touch the "Stopwatch" icon along the bottom row.

This is a very simple App. To start the stopwatch, tap the "**Start**" button and the clock will start to run.

Showing "Lap" times

You can either "Stop" or "Lap" the stop watch after you start it.

Just touch the "Lap" button is you were timing a sporting event like a track race.

Each "lap" time is shown in the list. Drag them up/down to see all the lap times.

When done, tap "Stop."

Stopping and Resetting

 Touch the red "Stop" sign to stop the clock at any time.

You can then continue the timing by touching "Start"  again.

Or touch "Reset" to reset the clock back to zero.

Using the Countdown "Timer" feature

Need to take something out of the oven in 30 minutes?

Need to take the pasta out in 8 minutes, but don't have any kitchen timer available?

Need to remember to turn off the sprinkler in 1 hour?

All these are perfect reasons to use the Timer which gives you a great count-down timer.

To set the Timer

Tap the Timer soft key inside the clock icon to see the timer screen.

Slide the dials at the top with your finger, setting the hours and / or minutes. In the screenshot to the right, we have the timer set for 30 minutes.

To change the sound you hear when the countdown timer reaches 0:00, touch the "When timer Ends" tab.

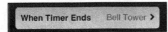

To change the sound you hear when the countdown timer reaches 0:00, touch the **"When timer Ends"** tab.

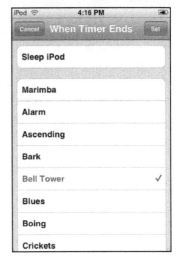

Turning Off ("Sleeping") your iPod after a Set Time

A great thing to be able to do is to set your iPod to turn off (go into sleep mode) at a set time.

Say you want to have your music play for 30 minutes and then turn off automatically. This is a good thing to set when you are going to sleep and want to listen to music but don't want to be bothered turning off your iPod.

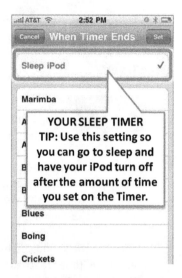

YOUR SLEEP TIMER TIP: Use this setting so you can go to sleep and have your iPod turn off after the amount of time you set on the Timer.

Start the Timer

Once you have the time and sound set, just touch the green "**Start**" button to start the timer.

The screen will display a digital clock counting down to zero. You can cancel the timer at any time by simply touching the red "**Cancel**" button.

Calculator App

One more very handy App included on your iPhone is the "Calculator" App. The iPhone Calculator can handle almost anything a typical family can throw its way; performing both basic and scientific calculations.

314

Viewing the Basic Calculator (Portrait Mode)

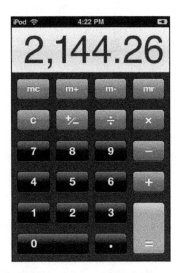

Click on the Calculator icon to start the Calculator App.

In Portrait mode (Vertical) view, the Calculator application is a "basic" calculator. All functions are activated by simply touching the corresponding key to perform the desired action.

Need to store something in memory?

M+ to add it into memory.
M- to subtract the number from memory,
MC to clear memory, and,
MR to recall the number in memory to the screen.

Viewing the Scientific Calculator (Landscape Mode)

Just turn the iPhone sideways into "Landscape" mode (horizontal) view and the accelerometer in the iPhone transforms the calculator into a "Scientific" calculator. The keys become smaller and the new "Scientific" keys are added along the left hand side of the calculator.

Turn your iPhone on its side to see this scientific calculator.

Turn the Calculator back to its vertical position and the calculator will return to its basic functions.

The Weather App

The iPhone comes with a very useful and easy to use "Weather" App built in.

After you set it up, a quick touch of the "Weather" icon will show you the next 6 days of weather forecasts for your area.

It is easy to setup your location and other locations to check their weather on the Weather Icon.

Getting Started with "Weather"

Tap Just touch the "**Weather**" icon. Unless you live in Cupertino, California, the default weather settings are not for your area. You will need to add your location. Touch the small "*i*" in the lower right hand corner to the Weather settings screen. If the town selected is not one you wish to keep track of, just touch the red "minus" sign and you will be prompted to "**Delete**" the location.

Adding a New Location

Just touch the "plus" sign in the upper left corner to add a new location.

Type in the name of the city or town (the iPhone will start to display towns it thinks you are trying to type.)

If it does not display suggestions as you type, touch "**Search**" after you type in your town.

When you see the town you want, you just touch it.

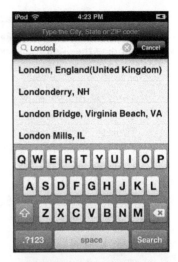

You will be taken back to the Weather settings screen.

If it looks OK to you, just touch "**Done**" in the upper right hand corner.

To Delete a Weather Location

To delete a weather location, first get into the Weather settings screen by tapping the "i" in the lower right corner of the weekly weather screen.

Then tap the red minus sign to the left of the location name so you see the "Delete" button appear. Finally, tap Delete and confirm to remove the location.

Tap "**Done**" in the upper right corner to complete your changes.

Re-Ordering the Locations in Weather

You can re-order the locations so your most important location is first on the list.

To re-order entry, touch and drag the three bars you see to the right of each entry.

Drop or let go of the entry when you have it in the correct location.

Tap "**Done**" in the upper right corner to complete your changes.

Moving Between Weather Locations

Once you have "Weather" set up for your various locations, you can then "Swipe" from screen to screen seeing the weather in all the cities you chose.

Touch and drag your finger across the screen to advance to the various Weather locations.

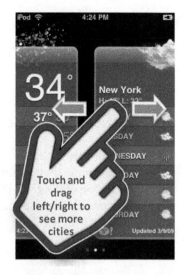

Chapter 22:
iTunes on your iPhone

Getting Started with iTunes on the iPhone

Earlier in this book we showed you how to get your music from iTunes on your computer into your iPhone along with Video and contact data (see page 84). One of the great things about iTunes is that it is easy to buy or obtain free music, videos, podcasts and audio books and use them in minutes right on your iPhone.

The iPhone allows you to access iTunes (the mobile version) right on the device. All you need is your cellular phone network connection or a Wi-Fi network connection in order to access the iTunes store. After you purchase or request free items, they will be downloaded to your iPod on the iPhone automatically transferred to your iTunes library on your computer the next time you perform a Sync.

How do you know when you can download Music, Videos and More from iTunes on your iPhone?

After you setup your iTunes account, you still need to have the right network connectivity to access iTunes and download media (music, videos, podcasts, more). Check out our Network Connectivity overview on page 19 and our Network Speed Overview on page 21 to learn more.

Starting iTunes

When you first received your iPhone, iTunes was one of the icons in the first Home screen page. Touch the iTunes Icon and you will be taken to the mobile iTunes Store.

NOTE: iTunes "App" does Change Frequently

Since iTunes is really a web site, it is likely to change somewhat between the time we wrote this book and when you are looking at it on your iPhone. In fact, one of the Soft keys on the bottom ("Top Tens") was moved up to the top row of 3 buttons has changed from "What's Hot" to "Top Tens" between the time when we started writing this book and when we completed it.

Navigating iTunes

iTunes uses similar icons to other programs on the iPhone, so getting around is quite easy. There are three buttons at the top and five icons or soft keys at the bottom to help you. You can even customize these soft keys - see page 326.

Scrolling is just like scrolling in any other program; just move your finger up or down to look at the selections available.

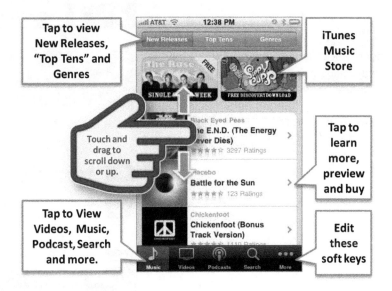

New Releases, Top Tens, and Genres

Along the top of the iTunes music store screen are three buttons; "New Releases," "Top Tens" and "Genres." By default, when you start iTunes you are shown the New Releases.

TOP TENS - "THE POPULAR STUFF"

If you like to see what is popular in a particular category, you will want to browse the "Top Tens" category. Tap "Top Tens" at the top, then tap a category or Genre to see what is popular for that category.

One note - these songs or videos are selling well - it doesn't mean that they will appeal to you. Always give the item a "Preview" and check out the "Reviews" before you pay for it.

Touch "**Rock**" and you can see the top ten songs or albums in the "Rock" category. The initial view shows you the "**Top Songs**."

To switch the view to "Top Albums," just touch the "**Top Albums**" button.

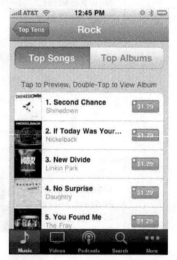

GENRES - "TYPES OF MUSIC"

Touch the "**Genres**" button to browse music based on genre. This is particularly helpful if you have a favorite type of music and would like to browse just that category.

The five most popular "Genres" are displayed, but you can touch on "**More Genres**" to see many more categories.

Go ahead and browse through the music until you see something that you would like to preview or buy.

iTunes for Videos (Movies), TV Shows and Music Videos

Touch the "**Videos**" button on the bottom to browse all the video related items.

Then you can tap the buttons at the top to check out:
- Movies,
- TV Shows and
- Music Videos.

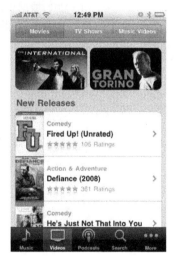

Tap on any movie or video to see more details and try the Preview.

RENTALS: Some videos and TV Shows allow you to "RENT" them for a set number of days.

BUY: This allows you to purchase and own the movie or TV show forever.

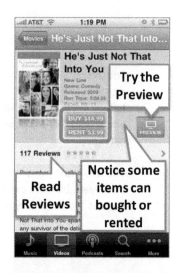

Tap anywhere in the "**Reviews**" line to check out all the reviews for this particular movie or TV show.

BEWARE OF EXPLICIT LANGUAGE IN REVIEWS: Many of the reviews are 'clean,' however some do contain explicit language which may not be caught by the iTunes store right away.

When you're done checking out the Movies then tap the "**TV Shows**" button at the top to see what is available from your favorite shows.

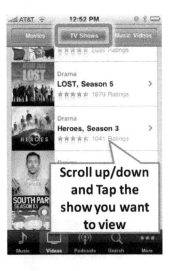

When you tap on a TV Series, you will then see the individual episodes available. Tap any episode to check out the 30-second preview. See page 189 for more on watching videos. When done with the preview, tap the "Done." button.

When you are ready to buy, you can choose to buy an individual episode or the entire TV series. Many, but not all TV Series, allow you to purchase individual episodes.

Maybe you want to get your fix of "Heroes" and see the Season 3 - Episode 2 that you missed. You can do it quickly on your iPhone.

Customizing Your iTunes Soft Keys

Just like in your iPod and other applications, you can customize the soft keys along the bottom of iTunes to fit your needs.

Let's say you love Audio books and wanted to put this soft key on the bottom for easy access. You also don't use Podcasts that much, so you want to replace "**Podcasts**" with the "**Audiobooks**" icon.

First, touch "**More**" at the bottom right corner. Then, drag and drop the "**Audiobooks**" icon to a position in the bottom icon bar. The icon you drop it on will be replaced. You can only have 4 icons + "More."

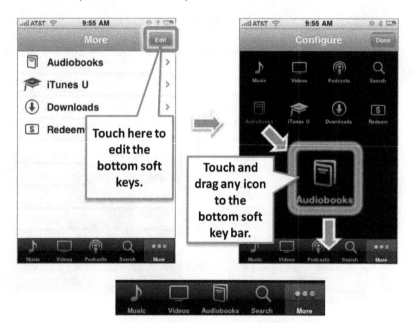

When you are finished with your changes, press "**Done**" in the upper right corner to save your changes.

NOTE: If you press the Home key at the bottom of the iPhone, your changes will be lost.

Audio Books in iTunes

If you are an audio book aficionado, be sure to check out the audio books in iTunes. If you don't see the Audiobooks icon at the bottom, touch the "More" icon then tap "Audiobooks."

Now you can use the top three buttons to browse the Audiobooks in iTunes:
- Featured,
- Top Tens, and,
- Categories.

Podcasts in iTunes

Podcasts are usually a series of audio segments, that may be updated frequently (like hourly news reports from National Public Radio), or not updated at all (a recording of a one-time lecture on a particular topic).

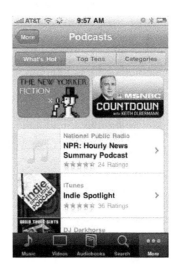

 If you don't see the "**Podcasts**" icon on the bottom row of soft keys, then touch the "**More**" icon then tap "**Podcasts**."

Now you can use the top three buttons to browse the Podcasts in iTunes:
- What's Hot,
- Top Tens, and,
- Categories.

"iTunes U" - Great Educational Content -

If you like educational content, then check out "iTunes U". You will be able to browse to see if your university, college or school has their own section.

One good example we discovered in just a few minutes of browsing around in "iTunes U" > "Universities & Colleges" > "Boston University" > "BUNIVERSE - Business" > "Audio" was a panel discussion with three Nobel Prize winning economists moderated by Paul Solmon (Economic correspondent for the PBS News Hour.) Like much of the content in iTunes U, it was **FREE**!

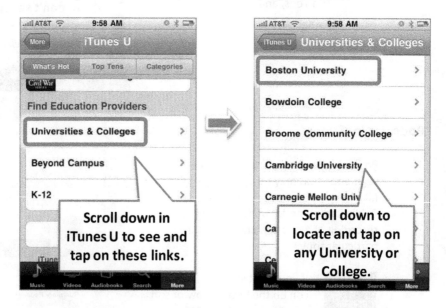

If you are in a location with a good wireless signal, just tap the title of the audio or video item and you can listen or watch it streaming

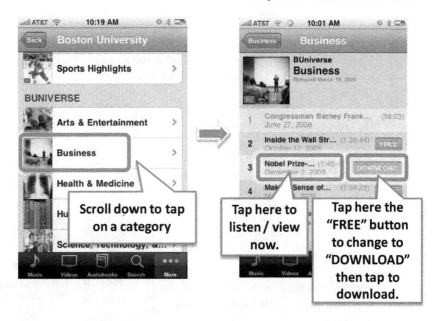

DOWNLOAD FOR OFF LINE VIEWING:
If you know you are going to be out of wireless coverage for a while, say on an airplane or in the subway, you will want to download the content for later 'off line' viewing or listening. Tap the "**FREE**" button to change it to a "**DOWNLOAD**" button and tap it again. You can then monitor the download progress (some larger videos may take 10 minutes or more to complete) by tapping the "**More**" soft key at the bottom, then tap "**Downloads.**" When the download is complete, the item will show up in the correct area in your iPod icon.

Searching iTunes

Sometimes, you have a good idea of what you want but are unsure where it is located, or you don't feel like "browsing" or navigating all the menus. The "Search" tool is for you.

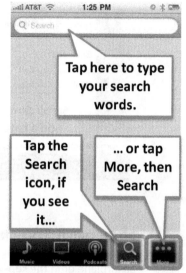

 Unless you have removed it by customizing your soft keys at the bottom (see page 326), you should have a magnifying glass - this is the "**Search**" icon.

Touch "**Search**" and the search window (familiar from other programs) comes to the top. Tap the search window and the keyboard will activate for you to type your search.

Tap here to type your search words.

Tap the Search icon, if you see it...

... or tap More, then Search

Type in the artist, song name, video name, podcast name, or album you are searching for and the iPhone will display matches. Be as general or as specific as you would like. If you are just looking to browse all particular songs by an artist – type the artist's name. If you want a specific song or album, enter the full name of the song or album.

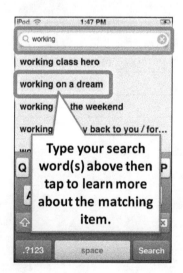

Type your search word(s) above then tap to learn more about the matching item.

When you locate the song or album name, simply touch it and you will be taken to the "Purchase" page.

Purchasing or Renting Music, Videos, Podcasts and More

Once you locate a song, video, TV show, or album, you can touch the "**BUY**" or (if you see it) the "**RENT**" button. Then your media will start downloading.

We suggest you view or listen to the "**preview**" and check out the customer "**Reviews**," unless you are absolutely sure you want to purchase the item.

Previewing Music

 Touch either the title of the song or the "Album Art" to the left of the Song title and the Album Cover will flip over and the preview window will launch. You will hear the first 30 seconds of the song.

Touch the "**Stop**" button and the Album Art will again be displayed.

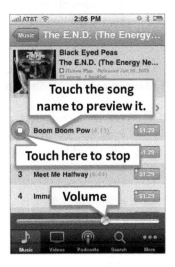

Check out Customer Reviews

Many items in iTunes offers customer reviews. The reviews range from a low of 1 star to a high of 5 stars.

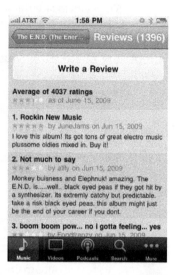

BEWARE OF EXPLICIT LANGUAGE IN REVIEWS: Many of the reviews are 'clean,' however some do contain explicit language which may not be caught by the iTunes store right away.

Reading the reviews will give you a fairly good idea of whether or not you would like to buy the item.

Previewing a Video, TV Show or Music Video

Pretty much everything on iTunes offers a Preview. Sometimes you will see a "Preview" button, like on Music Videos and Movies. TV shows are a little different, you tap the episode title in order to see the 30 second preview.

We do highly recommend checking out the reviews as well as trying the preview before purchasing on iTunes.

Typical movie previews or "trailers" will be longer than 30 seconds - some are 2 minutes 30 seconds or longer.

Purchasing a song, video or other item

Once you are sure you want to purchase a song, video or other item, touch the price of the song or the "**BUY**" button.

The button will change and turn into a green "**BUY NOW**" button.

Tap the "**BUY NOW**" button.

You will see an animated icon jump into the shopping cart. Type in your iTunes password and touch "**OK**" to complete the sale.

The song will then become part of your music library and will be synced with your computer the next time you connect your iPhone to iTunes on your computer.

After the download is complete, you will see the new song, video or other item inside the correct category within your iPod icon. (See page 169 for help with using the iPod for music and podcasts and see page 188 for videos.)

Downloading Podcasts

Podcasts are usually "User recorded" shows, talks or discussions made available for free on iTunes. Touch the "**Podcasts**" icon in the bottom row to see available podcasts for download.
You will see the top row of buttons change in the "Podcast" menu to "**What's Hot**," "**Top Tens**" and "**Categories**."

Touch "**Top Tens**" and you will see the top Podcasts in many of the categories ranging from News and Politics to Comedy.

Touch the "**Categories**" button to browse through the available Podcast Categories.

Downloading a Podcast

Podcasts are available in Video and Audio varieties. When you locate a Podcast, just touch the tab. Luckily, most Podcasts are free. If it is free, the typical "**Buy**" button will just say "**Free.**"

When you touch the button, it turns into a green button that says "**DOWNLOAD.**" Touch "**DOWNLOAD**" and an animated icon jumps down into your "**MORE**" or "**DOWNLOADS**" icon at the bottom bar of soft keys. A small number displayed in red reflects the number of files downloading.

The Download Icon - Stopping & Deleting Downloads

As you download items, they appear in your "Downloads" screen. This is just like iTunes on your computer.

Touch the "Downloads" icon along the bottom row to see the progress of all your downloads.

Where do the downloads go?
All your downloads will be visible in your iPod icon organized by the category. In other words, if you downloaded a Podcast, you will need to go into your iPod icon and touch the "Podcasts" icon on the bottom to see the downloaded podcast.

Sometimes, you decide that you do not want the all downloads you selected. If you want to stop a download and delete it, swipe your finger over the download to bring up the **DELETE** button. Then tap "**DELETE**."

Swipe your finger on the download

Tap here to stop and delete the download

Redeeming an iTunes Gift Card

One of the cool things about iTunes on your iPhone is that just like with iTunes on your computer, you can redeem a gift card and receive credit in your iTunes account for your purchases.

If you have customized your soft keys at the bottom (see page 170), you may see the "**Redeem**" soft key. If not, tap the "**More**" soft key in the lower left corner, then tap the "**Redeem**" button.

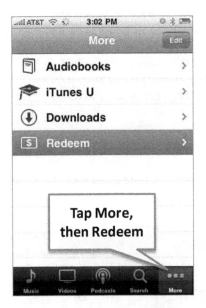
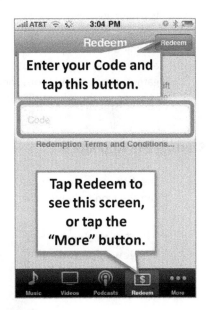

You will then be prompted to enter in your iTunes Gift Card info or Gift Certificate info in the box. Once successfully input, you will have credit for downloads in the iTunes store – it is that easy!

Chapter 23:
The Amazing App Store

We have just seen how easy it is download music, videos and
podcasts from iTunes right on your iPhone. It is just as easy to
download new applications from the Apple "App" store. "Apps"
are available for just about any function your could think of –
games, productivity tools, social networking – whatever you can
imagine, as the advertising says: "There's an App for that.

Starting the App Store

The App Store icon should be on your first page of icons on the Home Screen.
Tap the icon to launch the "**App Store.**"

Like iTunes, the "App Store" has buttons on top and soft keys at the bottom
which help direct you in your purchases.

Along the top, there are buttons for "**New**" Apps and "**What's Hot.**" Along the bottom are icons for "**Featured**," "**Categories**," "**Top 25**," "**Search**" and "**Update.**"

Scrolling is handled the same way as in iTunes and in other programs – just move your finger up and down to scroll through the items.

How do you know when you can download Apps from the App Store on your iPhone?

After you setup your App Store (iTunes) account, you still need to have the right network connectivity to access the App Store and download Apps (both large and small). Check out our Network Connectivity overview on page 19 and our Network Speed Overview on page 21 to learn more.

Finding an "App" to Download

Begin by looking around the default view – which is the "**Featured**" Apps. The App store loads with the "New" apps showing first. Just scroll from top to bottom to view all the new Apps in the store.

Change view to "What's Hot"

Touch the "**What's Hot**" button on the top and the "hottest" Apps in the store will now be visible on the screen. Again, just scroll through the "hot" apps to see if something catches your eye.

Using "Categories"

Sometimes, all the choices can be a bit overwhelming. If you have a sense of what type of App you are looking for, touch the "**Categories**" button along the bottom row of icons.

The Apps are now in "**Category**" tabs, ranging from "**Games**" to "**Medical**" and all sorts of other possibilities.

Find the Category of what you are searching for and touch the tab. So, if we knew we were looking for a "Game," we would just touch the "**Games**" category. W can then pick a sub-category like "**Action**" or "**Sports**."

Scroll through the options until you find a "Game" you want to download onto your iPhone.

Looking at the "Top 25"

Touch the "**Top 25**" icon along the bottom row and the App store will change the view again; this time showing you the top 25 Paid and top 25 Free Apps. Just touch "**Top Paid**" or "**Top Free**" to switch between the views.

Searching for an App

Let's say you have a specific idea of what you are looking for. Touch the "**Search**" icon and type in either the name of the program or the type of program you are looking for.

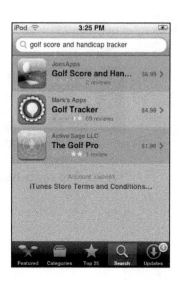

So, if you were looking for a Golf Scorecard program, just type in "Golf" or "Golf Scorecard" and see what comes up. When you see something that resembles what you are searching for come up in the screen, just touch it.

Downloading an App

Once you find the App you are looking for, you can download it right onto your iPhone.

Locate the App you want to buy and notice the small button that either says

"**FREE**" or "**$0.99**" (or whatever the price is.) Just touch that button, and it will change to say "**Install**" if it is a free program or "**Buy Now**" if it is a

paid program.

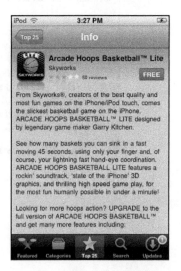

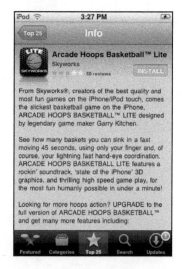

If you are sure that you want to purchase/install the App, just touch the button. You will be prompted to type in your iTunes password. When you are done, just touch "**OK**" and the App will start to download.

Finding Free or Discounted Apps

After browsing around you will notice a couple of things about the App Store. First, there are lots of FREE apps. Sometimes these are great applications, other times, they are not so useful - but are fun!

The other thing that you will notice over time is that some of the apps will have sales, and some apps will become less expensive over time. So if you have a favorite app and it costs $6.99, it is likely that waiting a few weeks or a month might result in a lower price.

Updating your Apps

Quite often, developers will "update" their Apps for the iPhone and iPhone. You don't even need to use your Computer to perform the update –you can do it right on your iPhone.

 Depending on how you have customized your soft keys on the bottom bar, you may see an "**Update**" icon. If you don't see the update icon, then tap the "**More**" button in the lower right corner to see it.

When you touch the Update button, the iPhone scans your device and then checks on line to see if updates are available. If they are, the Apps that need to update are shown on the screen.

To get your updates, you could touch an individual app, but it is easier to touch the "**Update All**" button to have all your Apps updated at once. The iPhone will leave the App store and you can see the progress of the update.

Chapter 24:
Fun on Your iPhone

Your iPhone excels at many things. It is a multi-media workhorse and it can keep track of your busy life as well. Two areas where the iPhone really excels are as a "Gaming Device" and "iPhone specific" versions of popular games.

Author's Note: We have written 9 books on the BlackBerry smartphones and have many BlackBerry devices 'laying' around the house. The BlackBerry smartphones don't disappear into our children's rooms, the iPhone is the only smartphone that our children have decided is fun enough to grab. We regularly discover that the iPhone has disappeared from its charger and have to yell out, "Where is my iPhone, I need to finish this book!"

iPhone as a "Gaming Device."

The TV ads tout it the iPhone as one of the "funnest" devices and it is true. Thanks to the built in accelerometer – essentially a device that detects movement (acceleration) and tilt – the iPhone is capable of doing thing that most portable game systems can't.

With the iPhone, you can play a driving game and use the iPhone itself to steer – just by turning the device. You can navigate a marble in a maze or a Motor Cycle on the road or a Monkey inside a ball just by turning and twisting the iPhone.

"Monkey Ball"

Tilt the iPhone to guide the Monkey in the ball

Or try a car racing game where you press the screen to accelerate or brake and tilt the iPhone left/right to turn the car - like a steering wheel.

The iPhone also has a very fast processor and a sophisticated graphics chip – bundle these with the accelerometer and you have a very capable "Gaming" device.

Where to Get Games

Games are found, just like all other Apps – at the App store – either through iTunes on your computer or on the App Store on the device.

Start up the App store, just as you did in the last chapter and use the "**Categories**" icon to bring you to the "**Games**" tab. Browse by Category – the "**Racing**" and "**Simulation**" and "**Arcade**" games see to have many of the games that take advantage of the accelerometer. You will also find many of these games in the "**Featured**" section of the App store as well.

Read Reviews Before you Buy

Many of the games have use reviews that are worth perusing. Sometimes, you can get a good sense of the game before you buy. If you find a game that looks interesting – don't be afraid to do a simple "Google" search on your computer to see if any mainstream media outlets have done a full review.

Look for "Free Trials" or "Lite" Versions

More and more, game developers are giving users free trials of their games to see if they like it before they buy. You will find many games have both a "Lite" version and a "Full" version in the App store.

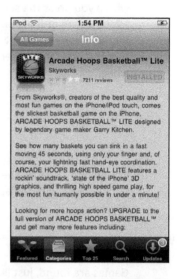

Be Careful when you Play

Some of the games actually let you use the iPhone as Bowling ball or golf club, or, in one of our favorite games, as a fishing rod. It is very easy when you "cast out your line" to also cast off or throw the iPhone – be sure you have a tight grip when you play these very fun games.

BEWARE - We have a friend with a 4-year-old who admits she is addicted to "Flick Fishing" seen in this image!

"Flick Fishing"

Flick the iPhone to cast.

Wind your finger to reel in your fish

iPhone Specific Versions

Because of the "Uniqueness" of the iPhone, many popular web sites and developers have created "iPhone Specific" versions of their sites or programs. Many are available for free in the App Store.

Newsreaders

Many in search of "News" will go first to
the New York Times Web site. Did you
also know that there is an iPhone specific
New York Times program? Just go to the
App store and search in the "News"
category.

Look under the "**Top Free**" programs and
you will find Newsreaders from not only
the New York Times., but also the
Associated Press, USA Today, ABC, NPR
and more.

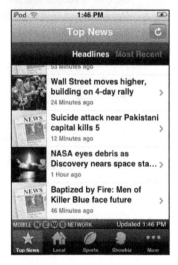

Each has a design and feel that looks just like your typical iPhone/iPhone
menus.

Social Networking

Are you a fan of facebook ™ or MySpace ™ or AIM ™ or other Social Networking site? Chance are that there is an "iPhone specific" version of your favorite web application – made just for the iPhone or iPhone.

Go to the App store and start browsing the categories. Choose "Social Networking" and then look under the "Free" applications or "Paid" applications.

Just as you did before, when you find the program you wish to download, touch either the "**Free**" button or the "**Buy Now**" button and the application will install on your iPhone.

Just touch the icon and the application usually asks for your login information and you are set to go.

YouTube on your iPhone

Watching YouTube videos is certainly one of the most popular things for people to do on their computers these days. Fortunately, this is one activity that you can take "on the road" with you. YouTube is as close to you as your iPhone.

Right on your Home screen is a YouTube icon. Just touch the YouTube icon and you will be taken to the YouTube App.

Searching for Videos

When you first start YouTube, you usually see the "**Featured**" videos on YouTube that day.

Just scroll through the video choices as you do in other Apps.

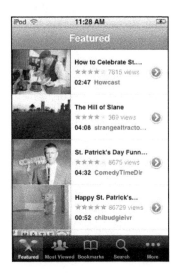

Using the Bottom icons

Along the bottom of the YouTube app are five icons; "**Featured**," "**Most Viewed**," "**Bookmarks**," "**Search**" and "**More**." Each is fairly self-explanatory.

To see the videos that YouTube is "Featuring" that day, just touch the "**Featured**" icon. To see those videos that are "**Most Viewed**" online- just touch the "**Most Viewed**" icon.

After you watch a particular video, you will have the option to set it as a "**Bookmark**" on YouTube for easy retrieval later on. If you have set bookmarks, they will appear when you touch the "**Bookmark**" icon.

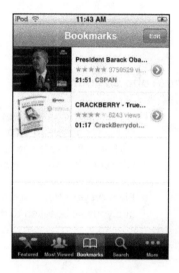

You can search the huge library of YouTube videos by touching the "**Search**" icon. Just touch the search box as in previous Apps, and the keyboard will pop up. Type in a phrase, topic or even the name of a video.

In this example, I am looking for the YouTube Video of the President's inauguration speech – so I just type in "Obama" and I see the list of videos to watch.

"More" Options

Just touch the "**More**" icon and you see a tab for "**Most Recent**," "**Top Rated**" and "**History**." Your YouTube App will keep track of what you watch and allow you to rate it, bookmark it and keep track of it.

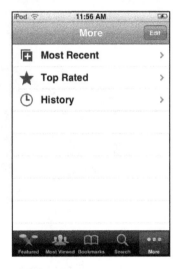

YouTube videos are rated by users on a scale of one to five stars. When you touch "**Top Rated**" you will see five start rated videos appear first.

Playing Videos

Once you have made your choice, just touch the video you want to watch. Your iPhone will begin playing the YouTube video in "Landscape" mode.

Video Controls

Once the video begins to play, the on screen controls disappear so you just see the video. To stop, pause or activate any other options while the video is playing, just tap the screen.

The on screen options are very similar to watching any other video. Along the top is the Slider showing your place in the Video. To move to another part in the Video, just drag the slider.

To Fast Forward through the video, just touch and hold the Fast Forward arrow. To quickly move in reverse, just touch and hold the Reverse arrow. To advance to the next Video in the YouTube list, just tap the Fast Forward/Next arrow. To watch the previous video in the list, just tap the Reverse/Back arrow.

To set a Bookmark – touch the "**Bookmark**" icon. To email the video, just touch the "**Mail**" icon and your email will start with the link to the video in the body of the email. Just input the recipient as you did on Page 274 when you sent a picture via email.

Additional Post-Viewing Options

When you are done watching the video, just touch the "**Done**" button. The next screen shows the full description of the video you just watched. You also have the option to send the video link (via email) once again by touching the "**Share**" button in the middle of the screen.

You can also scroll down the screen and see "**Related Videos**" to the one you were just watching.

Checking and Clearing your History

Touch the "**More**" icon in the lower right hand corner and then touch the "**History**" tab. Your recently viewed videos appear. If you want to "**Clear**" your history, just touch the "**Clear**" button. To watch a video from your history, just touch it and it will start to play.

Chapter 25:
Fixing Problems

The iPhone is a normally highly reliable. Occasionally, like your computer or any complicated electronic device, you might have to "reset" the device or troubleshoot a problem.

How do I know when I have the correct network connectivity for email, web browsing, the App Store downloads on my iPhone?

You need specific network connectivity for email, web browsing and App Store downloads to work on your iPhone. Check out our Network Connectivity overview on page 19 and our Network Speed Overview on page 21 to learn more.

What to do if the iPhone Stops Responding

Sometimes, your iPhone won't respond to your touch – it freezes in the midst of the program. If this happens, the first thing to do is try to push the "Home" button and get out of the program.

If this does not work – make sure you iPhone isn't running out of power – try plugging it in or attaching it to your computer (if it's plugged in) and see if it will start to respond.

If the iPhone continues to be unresponsive, try holding the "Home" button for about six or seven seconds – this should "quit" the program.

If holding the "Home" button doesn't work, you will need to "Power Down" your iPhone.

First things to try when your iPhone becomes unresponsive.

4. Press and hold for 3-4 seconds to power off.

1. Tap once to try and exit unresponsive program.

2. Press & hold for 6-7 seconds to try to force the exit.

3. Try to connect to your computer or power source.

After you power-off the iPhone, wait a minute or so and then turn on the iPhone by holding the same "Power" button for a few seconds.

You should see the Apple logo appear on the screen. Wait until the iPhone starts up and you should be able to access your programs and data.

If those steps don't work, you will need to "Reset" your iPhone.

How to Reset the iPhone

"Resetting" your iPhone is your last response to an "unresponsive" iPhone. It is perfectly safe, and usually fixes most problems.

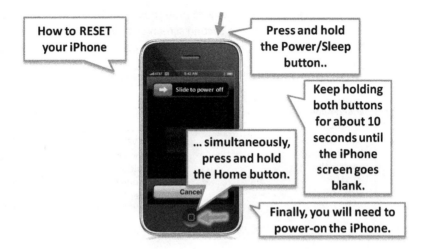

The way to "Reset" your iPhone is to use two hands and press and hold the "Home" button and the "Power/Sleep/Wake" button at the same time. Keep both buttons held down for about 8-10 seconds. You should then see the Apple logo appear. When you see the logo, just release the buttons and your iPhone will be reset.

Finally, you will need to power-on the iPhone.

Connect to iTunes Screen

As we covered in the chapters on iTunes, every iPhone is "Associated" with an iTunes account. It is that association that allows you to purchase music and Apps from your iPhone. It is also that "association" that allows you to play music from your iTunes account on your computer on your iPhone.

Sometimes, your iPhone might "lose" its registration and connection with iTunes. Usually, this is a very simple fix. Just connect your iPhone to the computer via the USB cable and iTunes will walk you through the process of "re-associating" your iPhone with your iTunes account.

iPhone Does Not Show Up in iTunes

Occasionally, when you connect your iPhones to your PC or Mac, your iPhone may not recognized in the iTunes screen.

In the first screen below, this is what you should see – your iPhone will be listed under "Devices." In the second screen shot, you will notice that there is no device shown – even though you iPhone is connected to the computer.

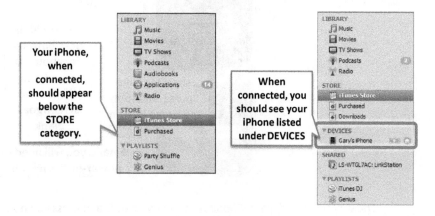

If this happens to you, the first thing to check is the battery charge of the iPhone. If you have let the battery run too far down, iTunes won't see it until the level of the battery rises a bit.

If the battery is charged, try connecting the iPhone to a different USB port on the computer. Sometimes, if you have always used one USB port for the iPhone and switch it to another port, the computer won't see it.

If this still does not fix the problem try disconnecting the iPhone and re-starting the computer. Then, reconnect the iPhone to the USB port.

If this still does not work, download the latest update to iTunes or completely uninstall and re-install iTunes on the computer again. Just make sure if you choose this option that you back up all the information in iTunes.

The latest version of iTunes can usually be found at: www.apple.com/itunes

Synchronization Problems

Sometimes, you might be having errors when Synchronizing your iPhone with your PC or Mac.

First, follow all the steps we outlined above on page 358 in the "iPhone Does Not Show Up in iTunes" section

If the iPhone still will not Sync, but you can see it in your iTunes directory, go back to the iTunes sync chapter starting on page 62 and check your the Sync settings very carefully.

Are you using Apple's "Mobile Me" program or "Microsoft Exchange?"
Microsoft Exchange is a push email and content program usually set up by an Enterprise Administrator. Mobile me is Apple's own "Wireless Sync" program that you can set up (for a fee) which will keep your information wirelessly in Sync. However, if you are using Mobile Me or Exchange, you won't be able to Sync through iTunes.

Go to your "Settings" icon from the home screen and scroll to the "Mail, Contacts and Calendars" tab and touch it.

If "Mobile Me" or "Exchange" is set up, it will show up in your list of "Accounts." If you don't see one of these on the list, then you are not using them to sync to your iPhone.

If you do see one of these items listed, touch the account and then "un-check" any categories or items that you would prefer to Sync through iTunes.

Now, when you go back into iTunes, those categories should show up as Sync options.

NOTE: If you do uncheck or "de-select" "Calendars" or "Contacts" in the "Mobile me" or "Exchange" accounts, you won't be able to see that information any more on the iPhone until you setup the synchronization from the computer via iTunes. (See page 92.)

No Sound in Music or Video

There are few things more frustrating than sitting down or moving about hoping to listen to music or watch a video and no sound comes out of the iPhone. Usually, there is an easy fix for this problem.

The first thing to do may seem obvious, but unplug your headphones (if you are using them) and then put them back in. Sometimes, the headset jack just isn't connected well.

If that doesn't fix the problem – check the volume. You might have accidentally lowered the volume all the way.

Next, make sure the song or video is not in "Pause" mode. Bring up the iPod music or video controls. Double-clicking the Home Button, should bring up the iPod music or video controls. (See page 179 for help.) Once you bring up the controls, verify the song is not PAUSED or the volume is not turned down all the way.

This symbol shows that the song is currently PAUSED. Tap to start playing.

This shows the volume is turned all the way down. Tap and drag to increase volume.

Next, check the "**Settings**" to see if you (or someone else) has set the "**Volume Limit**" on the iPhone.

Touch the "**Settings**" icon. Scroll down and touch "iPod" to see the screen shown.

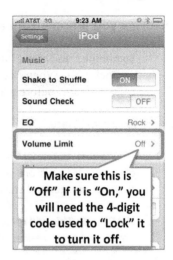

NOTE: If you don't have version 3.0 installed, in your Settings icon you may see a "**Music**" tab instead of "**iPod**," press "**Music**" in that instead.

The last item in the Music settings area is the "**Volume Limit**" tab – make sure it is set to "**Off**." If it is "On" then you need to check it and unlock it - you will need to know the 4-digit code used to originally lock it.

If none of these options help, bring your iPhone back to the place of purchase for repair.

If You Can't Make Purchases from iTunes or App Store

You have this new, cool device and you go to the iTunes Store or the App store and you are given an error message or not allowed to make a purchase – what do you do now?

The first thing to do is make sure that you have an active iTunes Account as we described on page 62.

Next, make sure you have an active wireless connection, either with the 3G cellular network or Wi-Fi connection. Look on page 18 to see what a network connection looks like on your iPhone (either 3G or Wi-Fi). Look on page 197 to see how to connect to a local Wi-Fi Network. While you can use your cell network – especially if you have 3G, having an active Wi-Fi connection will be much faster for downloading songs, videos, podcasts or "Apps."

Restoring you iPhone from a Backup

Sometimes, you might have to "restore" your iPhone to an earlier or even its original state. When all the troubleshooting is done and it still malfunctions, try a "Restore" before you decide to return your iPhone to the store.

Restore to Original State

The easiest, but most severe (because it erases all your data and apps), type of restore is to restore your device to its *original state*. Connect your iPhone to the computer and start iTunes, if it does not start automatically.

WARNING: This will totally "wipe" your iPhone clean – you will need to re-synchronize and re-install your Apps.

Click on the name of your iPhone under "**DEVICES**" in the left column. Now, you will see the iPhone information screen. You may need to scroll down the middle screen to see the "**RESTORE**" button as shown below.

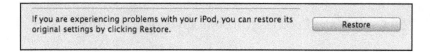

Click the "**Restore**" button and your iPhone will be restored to its original settings.

Restore from Previous Backup

The second kind of "Restore" is to try to restore from a previous backup. This is not as "clean" as a complete restore, but it will cut down on the time needed to get your iPhone loaded with all you music, videos and personal information.

Follow all the directions from above. After you have been prompted to tell you that you iPhone has been restored, you will be given the option to restore to a previous backup version or to set up new.

Choose "Restore from the Backup of" and then look in the drop down list for the most recent backup.

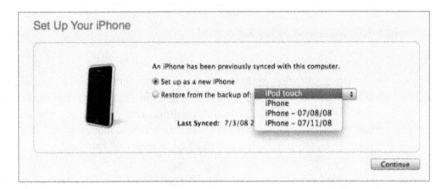

Chapter 26:
Upgrade your iPhone Software

Version 3.0 Software Now Released

As of the publication of this book, Apple has recently rolled out version 3.0 software to the public. If you have purchased your iPhone before about June 2009, it is very likely you are using version 2.x on your iPhone and you will need to upgrade to version 3.0. Many of the new features are things long asked for by iPhone users since the first iPhone was released.

How can you tell what version of software you are currently using on your iPhone?

Start your Settings Icon, then touch "General" then touch "About." Near the bottom of the "About" screen, you will see the version of software you are running on your iPhone. If it lower than 3.0, then you should follow the steps in this chapter to upgrade to the latest version.

TIP: You will also notice on the "About" screen that you can see how many Songs, Videos, Photos and Applications are loaded on your iPhone. You can also see how much of your total memory ("Capacity") you have left next to the word "Available."

Version 3.0 Software New Features and Enhancements

Below is a summary of the new features as well as the listing of a page or pages in this book on where to find more information about how to use this feature.

Copy and Paste

One feature iPhone features have always wanted is "Copy and Paste" – the ability to take text from one application and directly copy it into another. The "Copy and Paste" technique, is very intuitive, very slick and fun to use. See page 48.

MMS

Multi-Media Messaging is pretty much standard fare on most smartphones and some more basic cell phones. With 3.0 software, iPhone users now have the ability to send and receive picture messages, send voice notes and "Media rich" content to mobile phones. See page 151

Landscape Keyboard

Typing on the iPhone keyboard can be a little tricky since the keys are so small in the standard "portrait" orientation. With version 3.0, you can now type your emails and Notes in "Landscape" mode giving you a much larger keyboard to work with – a welcome addition. See page 48 .

Voice Memos

A new Native App is included in version 3.0 for recording Voice memos. A slick interface and the ability to "trim" the voice note and then send via email or MMS makes this a full feature application. See page 301.

Email Multiple Pictures

Previously, only one picture could be selected and sent to a contact. Now, you can select multiple pictures from the thumbnail view and send them via email or MMS. See page 155.

Installing the 3.0 Software Update

When the 3.0 Software update (or any future software update) is available, iTunes will let you know. Just plug your iPhone into iTunes as you usually do.

Your iPhone may say that it is version 2.2 or higher at the start of this process.

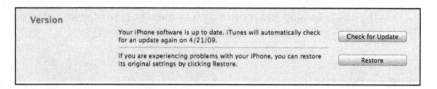

if the update does not start immediately, you can click on the "Check for Update" button located under "Version" on your iTunes screen as show below.

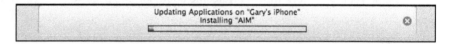

The first part of the Update Process is to back up your iPhone's data. This is a very important step since a firmware update completely erases your iPhone and installs new software and then restores your data.

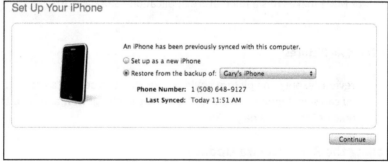

The Update process takes a while, you will receive progress information in the iTunes window. Once the software is installed, iTunes will then "restore" your Data.

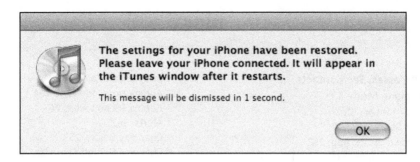

IMPORTANT NOTE: If you "Manually Manage" your music on your iPhone, your music and playlists will need to be "re-loaded" onto your iPhone as you did in chapter 2. See page 72

When the update is completed, your iPhone should now show that it is version 3.0.

> **Name:** Gary's iPhone
> **Capacity:** 7.08 GB
> **Software Version:** 3.0

INDEX

www.ingramcontent.com/pod-product-compliance
Lightning Source LLC
Chambersburg PA
CBHW071401050326
40689CB00010B/1712